THE REFERENCE SHELF   VOLUME 37 NUMBER 6

COLLEGES AT

THE CROSSROADS

EDITED BY

WILLIAM P. LINEBERRY

Senior Editor, Foreign Policy Association

THE H. W. WILSON COMPANY
NEW YORK   1966

THE REFERENCE SHELF

The books in this series contain reprints of articles, excerpts from books, and addresses on current issues and social trends in the United States and other countries. There are six separately bound numbers in each volume, all of which are generally published in the same calendar year. One number is a collection of recent speeches; each of the others is devoted to a single subject and gives background information and discussion from various points of view, concluding with a comprehensive bibliography.

Subscribers to the current volume receive the books as issued. The subscription rate is $12 ($15 foreign) for a volume of six numbers. Single numbers are $3 each.

PREFACE

"But now, at last, in this year of our Lord 1965, we have quit talking and started acting." So spoke President Lyndon B. Johnson in hailing passage of the Federal Higher Education Act of 1965, to which many of the nation's students and educators might have added a heartfelt "Amen!" His record-breaking $2.3 billion program provides funds for some 140,000 student scholarships, loans, and work opportunities and also expands Federal grant-in-aid subsidies for construction of college facilities and purchase of equipment. Through massive spending on research projects, the Federal Government's impact on the nation's colleges and universities is already great. Now, it is clear, that impact will broaden. For the President has emphatically let it be known that in his "Great Society" higher education will occupy a place of special distinction and importance.

The attention now being lavished by Federal authorities on one of the nation's oldest institutions has come at a critical time. For American higher education is currently undergoing one of its greatest transformations in history. A spectacular expansion is underway, heralded by a rising tide of youngsters clamoring for admittance at the gates of learning. The accumulation of knowledge, especially in scientific fields, is proceeding at an awesome and unprecedented pace. Once a relaxed, intimate community of scholars, the American college today is fast becoming a complex and sprawling community of specialists, administered by hundreds of executives, employing a thousand or more teachers and serving tens of thousands of students.

Such a transformation inevitably gives rise to momentous problems. Where will the money come from to finance rising enrollments? How can facilities keep pace with rapid expansion in various fields of knowledge? And at a time when the Federal Government itself is drawing off more and more of the nation's Ph.D.'s for its own research programs, where will the teachers be found to staff expanding faculties? Such questions merely scratch

3

the surface of the problems that must be overcome if higher education is to meet its responsibilities today.

This compilation is designed to examine the historic transformation that is taking place and to spotlight the problems that have arisen in its wake. The first section provides background: a history of the American college and a comprehensive survey of the contemporary changes underway. The second section explores some aspects of the current crisis, giving particular attention to the significance and meaning of the student revolt on the Berkeley campus of the University of California during the winter of 1964-1965.

The third section is devoted to an analysis of today's college student—his values, ambitions, attitudes, and interests. And in the fourth section consideration is given to the special pressures and problems experienced by faculty members. The compilation concludes with a brief epilogue which seeks to place the values and rewards of higher education in perspective.

A word about terminology: though technically a *college* is an institution granting only bachelor's degrees or certificates whereas a *university* is an institution (sometimes composed of various colleges and professional schools) granting graduate degrees, the two terms, for the purpose of this compilation, should be considered synonymous.

The compiler wishes to thank the authors and publishers who have courteously granted permission for the reprinting of their materials in this book.

WILLIAM P. LINEBERRY

November 1965

CONTENTS

PREFACE 3

I. TRANSFORMATION OF AN AMERICAN INSTITUTION

Editor's Introduction 9

James Bryant Conant. The American College: How It Grew   10

Clark Kerr. The Frantic Race to Remain Contemporary ...
.... Daedalus   26

II. SOME ASPECTS OF THE CURRENT CRISIS

Editor's Introduction 48

Andrew Hacker. The "Quality-Quantity" Crisis ....
.... New York Times Magazine   49

State Universities in Trouble ....
.... U. S. News & World Report   56

Roger Ricklefs. The Problem of Soaring Costs ....
.... Wall Street Journal   61

Serving Knowledge—Or the Government? ....
.... Business Week   65

Sheldon S. Wolin and John H. Schaar. Some Lessons from
    the Berkeley Crisis .... New York Review of Books   71

III. Today's Students: A New Breed?

Editor's Introduction   89

The Mood on Campus .... Newsweek   90

Changes in Today's College Students ....
.... U. S. News & World Report 111

Morton M. Hunt and Rena Corman. Students Under Stress:
    Emotional Conflicts .... Saturday Evening Post 118

IV. The Faculty: Pressures and Problems

Editor's Introduction 128

Bruce Dearing. Three Myths About the College Teacher ...
.... Saturday Review 129

John Fischer. Is There a Teacher on the Faculty? ....
.... Harper's Magazine 136

Lester E. Hurt. The Case Against "Publish-or-Perish" .....
.... NEA Journal 148

Norman S. Care. The Tenure Problem ..... New Republic 153

Robert Presthus. The Growth of Academic Bureaucracy ...
.... New Republic 158

Epilogue

Measuring the Value of Higher Education ....
.... First National City Bank Monthly Economic Letter 168

Bibliography 176

I. TRANSFORMATION OF AN AMERICAN INSTITUTION

EDITOR'S INTRODUCTION

The history of American higher education is the history of the phenomenal growth and development of a unique institution. The American college traces its origin to ancient British seats of learning, particularly Oxford and Cambridge universities. But in the modern world there is really nothing quite equal to it. In scope, function and purpose it stands alone, the extraordinary creation of the first society in history rich enough to afford the pursuit of knowledge on a mass basis.

Already more than 40 per cent of the nation's young men and women between the ages of eighteen and twenty-one attend college—a figure that has climbed rapidly over the past two decades and is expected to go on climbing rapidly in the decade ahead. In fact, the very success of American higher education, as reflected in its mass popularity, has become a source of critical problems as the crush of young applicants threatens to outstrip available facilities. At the same time pressures generated by the increasingly heavy demands of government and business on the academic community are adding to the general climate of distress. In short, American higher education is facing a crisis born of its own success. And in its frantic race to keep abreast of developments, its basic character is undergoing a major transformation.

This section examines the nature of that transformation and the historical conditions out of which it grew. In the first article, a distinguished educator, Dr. James B. Conant, traces the history of the American college from colonial times to the postwar period of contemporary ferment. He believes higher education has become diluted as it has spread and worries whether more and more youngsters may not be going to college for the wrong reasons.

In the second article the president of the University of California, Clark Kerr, sets forth the nature of the transformation that is currently taking place and analyzes the key forces working for change. He finds "four great areas of related adjustments: (1) growth, (2) shifting academic emphases, (3) involvement in the life of society, and (4) response to the new Federal involvement." Out of the contemporary chaos, he seeks to fashion a reasonably coherent picture of the direction higher education in America is taking.

THE AMERICAN COLLEGE: HOW IT GREW [1]

It has often been said that in the United States "everyone goes to college." This is far from the case, of course; less than a third of the potential students ... [as of 1953 were] enrolled either full time or part time in our colleges and universities. Nevertheless, as compared with the British nations, one might be tempted to make some such grossly exaggerated statement in order to emphasize the differences. . . . It would be just as fair to say in addition, "In England, Scotland, Australia, and New Zealand no one goes to college." For in the American sense of the word, no one does, for no such institution as the American college exists in any of the four countries. Oxford and Cambridge occupy today and have always occupied a special position. Their residential colleges provide a special kind of general education; in Oxford, in particular, certain combinations of studies (the Greats and the Modern Greats) offered a training that until recently at least was believed to be specially suitable for the future civil servant or politician. But aside from those two institutions, one can fairly say that the British universities are essentially professional schools, and, one should add, professional schools with the highest standards.

In Great Britain and the nations of the British Commonwealth in general, a boy or girl enters a university at age seventeen or eighteen or nineteen in order to obtain a professional

[1] Reprinted by permission of the publishers from James Bryant Conant, *Education and Liberty*. Cambridge, Mass.: Harvard University Press, Copyright, 1953, by the President and Fellows of Harvard College. p 29-54. Dr. Conant, one of the nation's leading educators and a former president of Harvard University, has made several studies of American education.

education; the specialized course of study is over and done with for the vast majority by the end of three or four years. In the United States, however, the elapsed time from the end of secondary school to a professional degree in law or medicine is five to eight years; even the bachelor's degree is with rare exceptions granted for not less than four years' study. Obviously it is not correct to say that in the United States a much larger percentage of our youth are attending a university than in British nations; for such a statement implies that the meaning of the word "university" is the same in all English-speaking countries, which is far from being the case. . . . A summary of the peculiarities of the picture in the United States might better be phrased in some such way as this: As contrasted to the British, Americans postpone specialization for several years (the study of engineering being an exception); a relatively large percentage of American youth start towards professional study but the fraction finally emerging with a completed professional training is not much greater than in the nations of the British Commonwealth. In short, it is the existence of that special phenomenon the American college that both increases the numbers of students enrolled in the first few years of advanced education and postpones the completion of professional training.

Our system of selecting professional students as compared with the British is like a long giant funnel narrowing down gradually. The British system, a generation ago at least, was more like a long narrow cylinder. Even today the analogy between a funnel and a cylinder holds because throughout the British system there is far more attempt to select the pre-university students at an early age than here in the United States. But whether my mechanical analogy is appropriate or not, it is evident that the size of our secondary school enrollment as well as the length of our post-high school education is closely linked to the nature of American colleges. Indeed, I should be inclined to argue that a major factor in the United States in forcing the expansion of free secondary schools has been the four-year liberal arts college. The drive for general education for *all* American youth has been the consequence, I believe, of the great popular success of the nonprofessional college with its relatively slight emphasis on selection of those with intellectual talents.

Let me make it plain that I am firmly convinced that this increasing demand for general education has been well founded. The "degree of instruction" required for all American youth in this complex civilization can only be met by increased concern with a broad type of schooling.

An Aristocracy of Talent

When Thomas Jefferson wrote of his desire to cull "the natural aristocracy of talents and virtue," and educate it "at the public expense, for the care of the public concerns," he was expressing what has become a premise of all democratic nations: namely, that the taxpayer has a duty to supply the talented with the education necessary for the development of that talent. Why? Because such educated talent will later serve the taxpayer by serving the entire nation. In theory at least, the application of this doctrine could lead to confining secondary education to those who are especially gifted in terms of "book learning" and only to those so talented. But even as great a democrat as Jefferson surely never had in mind denying opportunities for formal education to the adolescent sons of families who could afford to pay for whatever schooling they could find. At all events, neither on this continent nor anywhere in the British Empire in the nineteenth century did organized society attempt to make private secondary schools or colleges primarily schools for those of talent. Rather, the tendency was in the other direction. Private schools emphasized the importance of educating for life rather than preparing for a profession; religion was central to the educational process in many if not most Protestant church-connected schools as well as in the Catholic parochial schools. The life of the school and the importance of the playing fields, of the corporate spirit, and of loyalty were emphasized quite as much as the process of developing intellectual talent. So too by 1900 in the American college it was being said, "It isn't what you learn but the friends you make that matters."

By the mid-nineteenth century there were all sorts of private academies in the United States and an increasing number of privately endowed colleges. In Great Britain the old "Public Schools" were in process of revitalization, owing largely to the example of Arnold of Rugby. Their success . . . was not without its repercussions in the United States. . . . For when, early in this century, the ideas of social democracy emerged throughout the English-speaking nations, the example of the popularity of the private school and college for those who could afford them became one driving force for using taxpayers' money for purposes less selective than Jefferson had in mind.

Whether or not the reader agrees with my diagnosis of the social and political forces that have operated in the last fifty years, there can be no doubt of the transformation. . . . Forty years ago the pattern in this country was not far different from what it is today in the other English-speaking countries: the college enrollment was still only 5 per cent of the age group. By 1930, however, over 10 per cent of the eighteen-to-twenty-one-year-olds were enrolled in a degree-granting institution and by 1940 the percentage had risen to 15; the postwar figure after the tide of veterans has receded will probably be about 20 per cent. [In fact, it is now more than 40 per cent.—Ed.]

Clearly there has evolved on this continent an idea about the education of young men and women that is quite different from the ideas of the British in either Great Britain or the newer countries of Australia and New Zealand. The American college as a special type of institution has assumed a position of great importance. A "college education" has become accepted as a desirable experience and in this century degree-granting institutions have expanded in size enormously.

The Origin of the American College

To understand how the American concept of a liberal arts college arose, one must turn back the pages of history four hundred years, for all the educational patterns that I am comparing have a common origin, namely, late sixteenth-century England.

A symbol of basic unity of the Anglo-Saxon world is the position of Shakespeare in the hierarchy of values implied in the teaching of literature in almost every school and college throughout the United States and the British Commonwealth. It is no accident that we all place the writings of an Elizabethan dramatist at the top of the list of what "every schoolboy should know."

England under Queen Elizabeth anglicized the Reformation; this English version of Calvinism provided the cultural basis for the seventeenth century; and it is in the seventeenth century that American educational history begins to diverge from the rest of the Anglo-Saxon pattern. Indeed, I am inclined to argue the paradoxical thesis that the late sixteenth- and early seventeenth-century English ideas about education have been perpetuated here on the North American continent, and it was the mother country, not the offspring, that departed from the original six-teenth-century tradition.

What I have in mind is simply this: In the first half of the seventeenth century, before the Civil Wars, Oxford and Cam-bridge were serving as educational centers for many young men who were not destined for the learned professions. The Reforma-tion of the preceding century, while leaving the forms of educa-tion largely unchanged in these two ancient universities, had in-troduced the new spirit of the age. Theology, the admitted queen of the sciences in the Middle Ages, had become popularized. The same set of ideas that had opened the Bible to all also demanded that *all* should be able to read. . . . Puritan and Presbyterian alike sought to provide free schools.

The history of Oxford and Cambridge from the Elizabethan settlement of the English Church to the outbreak of the Civil War in 1642 is the history of institutions seething with intellec-tual and political excitement. The opportunity to read and dis-cuss the sacred writings bore fruit rapidly. The conflict between the High Church party and the Puritans that finally led to a clash of arms had been going on for at least three generations in the colleges of Oxford and Cambridge before the Long Parliament was called. One of the demands of the Puritan party was that "the two fountains of learning" be cleansed, that is,

COLLEGES AT THE CROSSROADS

purified from any leanings towards the Roman Catholic Church.

Not only were the English universities in the early seventeenth century exciting places, but they were extraordinarily well attended. Something like a thousand young men entered Oxford and Cambridge each year in the first half of the seventeenth century. When one considers that the total population was about five million, this means in terms of the age group that perhaps as many as 2 per cent of the young men were in attendance in these two universities (there were, of course, no others). After the Civil Wars the situation changed, and it is probably safe to say that not until the twentieth century did so high a proportion of the young men of England attend a university as in the first third of the seventeenth century.

The significant point is this. At the time to which I am directing attention, namely, the early decades of the seventeenth century, the role of the university was thought of not only in terms of training ministers, lawyers, doctors, but also in terms of educating gentlemen who were to take a leading part in public affairs. To document this statement would require a long digression. I shall not content myself by noting: first, the very large attendance at the universities, in itself evidence they were regarded as something other than theological and law schools; second the large number of laymen who played historic parts in the struggle between King and Parliament who were former Oxford and Cambridge students; third, the significance of Puritan Oxford as a center of the new "experimental philosophy" during the Cromwellian period; and fourth, the influence of Oxford and Cambridge men in the seventeenth-century settlements on the coast of North America.

As to the last point, some of the most striking evidence of the nature of Oxford and Cambridge education in the seventeenth century is provided by what was said by the founders of Harvard College. That a group of pioneers settling in a wilderness should have gone through with a scheme to start and operate a college within a generation of the settlement is a remarkable phenomenon. It is explicable only if one realizes how many Oxford and Cambridge men there were among the settlers. The English

Puritan tradition was supersaturated with learning; it is not surprising, therefore, that when this tradition was transplanted to New England, the crystallization of a new university at once took place. To be sure, the Puritans required a learned ministry; it is easy to exaggerate, however, the significance of the famous phrase about the necessity of providing ministers when those among the immigrants should "lie in the dust." As Professor [Samuel Eliot] Morison has demonstrated, it was not a theological seminary but the replica of a Cambridge college that the New England settlers sought to establish in founding Harvard. And through many ups and downs they and their descendants succeeded in keeping the college going, always with an eye on Oxford and Cambridge where so many of the founders had obtained their education.

An American Tradition Takes Shape

Now we come to the divergence of the two streams—one American, the other British. The second half of the seventeenth century is to my mind the watershed between education in this country on the one hand and the educational tradition of all the rest of the English-speaking world on the other. Three significant events occurred in North America that have profoundly influenced all subsequent developments in the area that is now the United States. Oxford in 1648 and later Cambridge, both under Puritan control, recognized the Harvard A.B. as equivalent to their own degree; they admitted Harvard graduates to the Oxford and Cambridge A.M. without further examination. Second, the College of William and Mary was chartered in 1693 and though the charter contains no explicit right to confer degrees, the implicit right must have been recognized in London, for degrees were awarded without question from the start. Third, in 1701 (I stretch the seventeenth century a bit) the Connecticut General Court chartered Yale and in so doing provided for the conferring of degrees. Then in the middle of the eighteenth century three other institutions for the granting of degrees were chartered in North America: Princeton in 1746 by the Governor of New Jersey, Columbia (King's College) in 1754 by George II, and the University of Pennsylvania (College, Academy and Charitable School) in 1755 by "the proprietors and governor in chief of the Province of Pennsylvania."

Thus by the middle of the eighteenth century there were six colleges in the North American colonies granting at least the first degrees in arts. Yet none of these institutions could be regarded as a true university because none had a faculty capable of examining for the higher degrees, at least by English and Continental standards. A precedent had been established that was to have a revolutionary effect on education. In the North American colonies the practice had become common for a college to grant the bachelor's degree to its graduates without reference to any other body of learned men. America had started down the road which in the twentieth century has led to the situation where American academic degrees are almost without meaning; the mere fact that an institution is a chartered college or university today in the United States is no guarantee of the quality of the instruction offered.

Six degree-granting colleges were established in North America by 1750, with apparently no protest from the mother country and no interest shown there in copying the new practice of the offspring. Probably what was happening across the Atlantic Ocean about such strictly academic matters as curricula and degrees excited no interest in London. The traditional guardians of the English degrees, Oxford and Cambridge, were enjoying what has been called "the corrupt sleep of the eighteenth century." If they had protested, the action of those same guardians in recognizing Harvard in 1648 might have been cited as a precedent against them. At all events, in the colonies, colleges granting degrees were established with no controls; at home Oxford and Cambridge continued unchallenged, except for the Scottish universities and Trinity College, Dublin, which had been chartered under Elizabeth.

The British University Tradition

The monopoly of the two ancient seats of learning on the Isis and the Cam remained unbroken until the University of

London was chartered in 1836. It not only remained unbroken but was narrowly confined by the Clarendon Code of the Restoration settlement (1661). Only those who subscribed to the doctrine of the Established Church were allowed to take degrees; with a few exceptions, only Church of England members were admitted even as students. As closed preserves neither Oxford nor Cambridge flourished. The dissenting academies that sprang up all over England in the mid-eighteenth century probably gave a much better education. It was in these academies rather than at Oxford and Cambridge that the seventeenth-century tradition of providing a gentleman's education was still vigorous. But of course these academies could not even think of granting degrees; they existed only by sufferance in a state formally committed to one church only.

Thus it came about that when in the early nineteenth century there was renewed interest in expanding education in English-speaking communities, the United States and Great Britain proceeded in quite different ways. Nothing was more natural than that each one of the thirteen sovereign states of the new nation should express its sovereignty by reincorporating the college or colleges already existing within its territory and by chartering new colleges with the right to grant degrees. Between 1780 and 1836 no less than eighty colleges and universities were founded in the United States and empowered by the state legislatures to award the bachelor's degree to their graduates. Most of these were independent corporations, many of them church-affiliated, but some were state universities, a new type of institution in the English-speaking world. During this same period in Great Britain, one and only one new university was chartered, the University of London. . . . And it was Oxford and Cambridge that largely determined the nature of London University.

The two ancient English universities had a consistent history of two centuries of fighting every effort to break their joint control of higher education. Even in the Cromwellian interlude this aspect of university life did not change, for we find a Puritan vice-chancellor of Oxford as vigorous in his opposition to establishing a new university at Durham as was his distant academic descendant in questioning the chartering of a university in London. When finally in 1836 after at least a decade of agitation, a degree-granting institution was established in the capital city of the British Empire, it was on the examining function of the university that stress was laid. University College, a completely secular college established in 1827, and King's College, a Church of England institution founded a few years later, became constituents of the new London University. Under the charter the University Senate, not the teaching bodies of either King's or University College, had the power to grant degrees based on adequate examination.

Britain Preserves High Standards

An important principle was here either established or reaffirmed (depending on how one reads the history of the two preceding centuries); this principle was that the degrees to be conferred in England were to conform as far as possible to the high standards set by Oxford and Cambridge. The doctrine was laid down that the granting of the bachelor's degree was not to be separated from the right and ability to grant higher degrees. The dissimilarity here with the American picture is evident. Every new university in England and throughout the British Commonwealth in the nineteenth century was destined to be primarily a collection of professional faculties carefully guarding the high standards of the degrees conferred.

One must remember that for the first half of the nineteenth century Oxford and Cambridge were still closed preserves and "unreformed." From 1850 to 1870 the Royal Commissions of Inquiry and the ensuing Parliamentary legislation were slowly adapting the two ancient institutions to new conditions. But it was not until the closing two decades of the nineteenth century that Oxford and Cambridge began to be considered by informed public opinion as leading modern universities. Relatively few of the graduates of the English "Public Schools" went on to these universities; thus the "Public Schools" were not essentially preparatory schools. Rather, to use a modern phrase, they "provided terminal education." To them was assigned the task of completing the education of those who would enter trade, industry, or public affairs. This idea of the role of the "Public Schools" was carried over to other parts of the British Empire in the second half of the nineteenth century, particularly to Australia.

Expansion of American Colleges in This Century

Here in the United States the course of history was quite different. As the nineteenth century wore on, degree-granting colleges more and more became the recognized media for maturing the leaders in all phases of public and commercial life. There was no restraining hand on experimentation with the curricula. Radical educational ideas could be introduced in the new Republic that were only discussed in England. Thomas Jefferson's proposals for the establishment of the University of Virginia is a case in point. The influence of what was projected in Virginia was felt in London. The Rockfish Gap Report of the Commissioners for the University of Virginia of 1818 was read and its revolutionary widening of the curriculum was eagerly welcomed by the London reformers. But when actually established and given authority to grant degrees, London University was still largely a reflection of the orthodox pattern of sound learning.

The multiplicity of colleges in the United States and the absence of restraints favored new ideas but also failed to encourage the maintenance of high standards. In spite of some valiant efforts to provide advanced instruction and attract eminent scholars, the American college of the 1850's was in fact not very different in intellectual accomplishment from a British "Public School." And it served much the same purpose. But note well two important differences, the results of a long history. The American college granted an A.B. degree, and the course of study was usually four years. To be sure, this did not mean necessarily four years' longer exposure to formal education for the American college student as compared with his British equivalent who finished a "Public School." For the students entered American colleges at a younger age one hundred years ago than they do today. But the idea of a bachelor's degree as the hallmark of a four-year course following twelve years of school work became firmly fixed in the minds of the educated classes in the United States.

By the closing decade of the century it had become increasingly fashionable to go to college. The degree-granting institutions, now numbering several hundred, were not professional schools; rather they were colleges preparing their students for nonprofessional activities. Their curricula, the organization of student life, their pedagogic methods were the resultant of a hundred years of American experience. A new type of educational institution had become firmly established. The American college, whether or not it called itself a university, by 1890 was both catering to and generating an enormous popular demand for what was then called a liberal education and now is known as general education. This demand was soon to affect not only the expanding colleges but the secondary schools as well.

Three factors must be borne in mind in analyzing American schools and colleges as they existed at the close of the last century. One was the growing belief that a college had a good deal to offer besides formal study; sports, fraternities, extracurricular life in general were already looming large in the minds of the alumni who were celebrating their twenty-fifth year out of college when the nineteenth century disappeared. Another is the fact that many a poor boy had been able to attend an American college in the nineteenth century by borrowing a little money from a relative and working at odd jobs and during the summer. That a man had worked his way through college was nothing to be ashamed of in the United States in 1900; on the contrary, it was a matter of great pride. No similar way of financing an education has obtained in the British Empire with the possible exception of Scotland. Even in this century the relation of education to remunerative work in British nations is different from what prevails in America.

Role of the Federal Government

The third factor directly influenced the American university rather than the American college, but had repercussions on the entire educational pattern. I refer to the Morrill Act of 1862 and the subsequent acts of Congress which made possible the land-grant colleges. Here the Federal Government was the pacemaker in providing public monies for advanced education. The different states applied the subsidy for "agricultural and mechanical arts colleges" in different fashions. Some founded new colleges that shortly became rivals of the existing state university; others used the money to strengthen the state university. Whatever route was used, opportunities for a very wide range of practical higher education were increasingly afforded in the seventies, the eighties, and the nineties. All this had its influence on the movement for extending the privilege of free education to ever-expanding numbers. If a subsidized college was to be available to teach the mechanical arts and agriculture, free schools had to be ready to prepare boys and girls for these colleges. Particularly in the Middle West this extension of public education assumed increasing importance as the twentieth century came in sight.

I shall not underline the obvious difference between the United States with its high geographic mobility and rapidly-expanding social structure on the one hand and the stratified immobilized society of Great Britain on the other. Nor need I emphasize the egalitarian spirit so characteristic of the United States as early as the 1830's. Both were of importance in bringing about the expansion of American education. . . .

Extending the Privileges of a College Education

If you combine a belief in equality with a belief in the desirability of a full-time education leading to a collegiate degree for all who can afford it, the American pattern of education is the logical outcome. In simple form, the question may be thus stated: if a British "Public School" education or an American college education is a "good thing" even for those who are not going to do university professional work, why isn't it a good thing for everyone? This question has been asked explicitly or implicitly by an increasing number of people in the United States and also, in the last thirty years, in Great Britain and the British Commonwealth. It should be noticed that these are quite different questions from the one to which Jefferson replied when he spoke of "culling the natural aristocracy of talents and virtue." He was answering the question: for whom is a special prolonged education to be provided at public expense? His answer is, only for those who are both talented and virtuous. But in increasing numbers the sons of the ruling class in Great Britain and the sons of the well-to-do in the United States were attending a "Public School" or a college whether or not they were talented and virtuous.

The English answer given in the Education Act of 1944 is essentially this: full-time education at public expense up to and through the university should be provided for the intellectually talented, part-time vocational education for the rest after they finish school at age sixteen. The British position is tenable only in a nation whose degree-granting institutions are highly selective and concerned chiefly with professional study. In the United States we have come perilously close to endorsing the view that a college education is a "good thing" for everyone; the only limitation has been expense, and working one's way through college has, for many, removed this hurdle. Having a multitude of colleges with no method of insuring any conformity to educational standards and emphasizing the nonintellectual side of college life, Americans could hardly claim that their colleges were selective. As to the lack of uniformity in regard to standards I may quote Henry Chauncey, President of the Educational Testing Service, who in reporting on the recent Selective Service tests has said, "A student who stands relatively low in one institution may compare very favorably, both in ability and in level of academic performance with a student who stands relatively high at another institution."

College education in the United States, as the twentieth century moved on, came to be more and more justified as a preparation for citizenship. It was more and more divorced from any

connection with professional training which was the province
of a university: law, medicine, theology, and gradually the sciences with the exception of engineering came to be regarded as
postgraduate subjects. The logical outcome of all this development was a continuous demand for a wide variety of new subjects to be taught in school as well as college. The drive for
general education—"education for citizenship'"—affected the high
schools even more than the colleges. At this point the expansion
of the high schools began—and their transformation. In less than
fifty years the pattern of full-time schooling . . . was completely
altered. . . .

Quest for "The Collegiate Way of Life"

By experimenting with various types of college courses, we
in the United States are attempting to find the modern equivalent of the kind of liberal education that was once the product
of "the collegiate way of life"—the ideal of the founders of the
first colleges in the colonial days. When literacy could be defined only in terms of languages, literature, and history, the
task of a college was relatively easy. An "education around the
dinner table" was, even in the nineteenth century, education
within a relatively narrow field of knowledge. Furthermore,
those who came to the universities then were already, for the
most part, from highly literate families. In England even a generation ago, the well-endowed residential colleges of Oxford and
Cambridge could enroll a majority of students from homes well
stocked with books. Today, however, I doubt whether anywhere
in the world the mere device of collegiate living (excellent though
such a way of life may still be for young men with intellectual
ambitions) suffices to provide the beginnings of a general education. The cultural background of the students is too diverse,
the impact of modern science and scholarship has been far too
great. These two factors have made necessary a reexamination of
the older idea of a liberal education.

General education cannot be dissociated from the family
background of the students. Furthermore, it cannot be wholly
dissociated from vocational ambitions. To reconcile this fact

with the desire to keep our youth as undifferentiated as possible at the high school age is one of the many really difficult problems facing the American high school. . . . The same problem arises in our colleges.

A ruthless critic might claim that much of what is offered to the American college student as general education is only highly vocational training dressed up in fancy academic language. To some degree such criticisms have validity. How far the development of special skills is a proper function of a university is an open question. Certainly few would care to defend such absurdities as courses in "fly casting" which count towards a degree. Our whole system of intercollegiate athletics with the emphasis on gate receipts and the recruitment of players is likewise open to ridicule by observers from other nations. The truth of the matter seems to be that in the vast chaotic mass of so-called "higher education" in the United States one can find almost anything one wishes either to praise or to condemn. As regards the numbers and diversity of institutions there is nothing faintly resembling it anywhere in the world. There are still many talented boys and girls who drop out of education far too soon; there are many less able who continue far too long. Yet on the whole, the American people applaud the American college and urge forward the drive for general education. . . .

The assumption that a general education on a full-time basis is a "good thing" for every youth who can afford it, when combined with the doctrine of "equality of opportunity," would appear to leave no logical alternative to a much further expansion of college education than has yet taken place even in the United States. Yet almost everyone is vaguely aware of certain difficulties in this argument. Are we sure that full-time education up to age twenty-one or twenty-two is beneficial for all types of individuals? Perhaps colleges after all were supposed to be concerned with developing intellectual talent; perhaps there should be some selection of the more rather than the less talented even among those who can afford to pay their way. Possibly, attempts to give a general education to the average good all-around boy at the college level interferes to some extent with the training of the "natural aristocracy of talents and virtue" to which Jefferson referred. It can even be argued by those who hold strongly to the egalitarian premise that less than four years of college together with part-time employment might provide the best education for many sons of the rich if it suffices for many children of the poor. What is needed, perhaps, is not an expansion of four-year college and university enrollment but a re-evaluation of what is the ideal education for different sorts of boys and girls irrespective of their family income. Possibly a four-year college education is no longer the privilege that those of us who are urging students to attend our institutions have so long assumed.

THE FRANTIC RACE TO REMAIN CONTEMPORARY[2]

"The true American University," David Starr Jordan once observed, "lies in the future." It still does; for American universities have not yet developed their full identity, their unique theory of purpose and function. They still look to older and to foreign models, although less and less; and the day is coming when these models will no longer serve at all.

The American university is currently undergoing its second great transformation. The first occurred during roughly the last quarter of the nineteenth century, when the land grant movement and German intellectualism were together bringing extraordinary change. The current transformation will cover roughly the quarter century after World War II. The university is being called upon to educate previously unimagined numbers of students; to respond to the expanding claims of government and industry and other segments of society as never before; to adapt to and channel new intellectual currents. By the end of this period, there will be a truly American university, an institution unique in world history, an institution not looking to other

[2] From article by Clark Kerr, president of the University of California. *Daedalus.* 93:1051-70. Fall '64. The article was adapted from the author's Godkin Lectures delivered at Harvard University in 1963 and published under the title *The Uses of the University.* Reprinted by permission of the publishers from Clark Kerr, *The Uses of the University.* Cambridge, Mass.: Harvard University Press, Copyright, 1963, by the President and Fellows of Harvard College.

models but itself serving as a model for universities in other parts of the globe. This is not said in boast. It is simply that the imperatives that are molding the American university are also at work around the world.

Each nation as it has become influential, has tended to develop the leading intellectual institutions of its world—Greece, the Italian cities, France, Spain, England, Germany, and now the United States. The great universities have developed in the great periods of the great political entities of history. Today, more than ever, education is inextricably involved in the quality of a nation. And the university, in particular, has become in America, and in other nations as well, a prime instrument of national purpose. This is new. This is the essence of the transformation now engulfing our universities.

American universities are currently facing four great areas of related adjustments: (1) growth, (2) shifting academic emphases, (3) involvement in the life of society, and (4) response to the new Federal involvement. The direction of adjustment in each of these areas is reasonably clear; the detailed arrangements and the timing are not. There are several other areas where adjustments will be necessary but where the direction of adjustment is as yet by no means clear; and four such areas will also be noted below.

Growth

The number of university and college students in the United States will almost double during the 1960's. This addition of three million will duplicate in one decade the growth of the three centuries since Harvard was founded. The proportion of graduate students will rise considerably, and there are already 25,000 postdoctoral students.

Existing university campuses are being enlarged and many new ones founded. The University of California, for example, now has seven campuses and a total enrollment of 65,000 students. Four of those campuses will triple or more in size in the next decade. One campus admitting undergraduates for the first time this fall, and two entirely new campuses admitting students for the first time in

1965, are being planned to accommodate ultimate enrollments of 27,500 each.

But university expansion alone cannot begin to meet the demand for some kind of education beyond the high school level. In the years before World War II, post-high school study was the exception; it is rapidly becoming the norm. In California today four out of every five high school graduates seek further education; soon it will be even more. This great shift in the pattern of American education will call for many more four-year colleges, both public and private. And a particularly large number of junior colleges will be formed as the community college movement becomes nationwide. Problems of differentiation of function will arise among public sectors of higher education—junior colleges, four-year colleges, and universities—as they compete for state support. The State of California has already met that problem through legislative adoption of a Master Plan for Higher Education, and other states are working along similar lines. However the total demand for higher education may be parceled out among the public and private institutions of varying types, one fact is clear: this will be the most unprecedented period of campus development in American history, or indeed in the history of the entire world.

To accommodate the great increase in enrollments, many academic calendars are being rearranged, particularly in state-supported institutions, to permit more nearly year-round use of physical facilities. Students will be able to accelerate their work if they wish, and general students will come and go with less reference to their "class"; more of them will drop in and drop out as suits their particular schedules and needs.

There will be some further mechanization of instruction (television, language laboratories, programed learning) to improve quality and to save faculty time for other endeavors, including more individual work with students. The sciences will almost eagerly embrace these aids to learning. The foreign language departments will be rather reluctant, because these devices can threaten their structure of faculty employment and the recruitment and utilization of graduate students.

Because of the competition for faculty members, salaries will continue to rise; fringe benefits of all sorts will be devised to tie professors to a particular campus. In addition to competition among universities, there is also intensified competition with industry and government. This competition has obvious advantages in raising faculty income, but it has its negative aspects. As the market becomes more active, internal equity will be injured, for some disciplines are much more in demand in the market than others. Teaching loads will be competitively reduced, sometimes to zero, although more teachers are needed and students are complaining about lack of attention. The identification of the professor with his university will be generally loosened—he will become more a member of a free-floating profession. The rules regarding how much time a professor can spend away from his university assignments, and those affecting the sources of his income within the university, will continue to be in great flux.

This current phenomenon of rising salaries and benefits, however, may be of relatively short duration, lasting, perhaps, for the remainder of this decade. Faculty salaries have been catching up with incomes in other professions after a historical lag. By 1970, also, the personnel deficit of today may be turning into the surplus of tomorrow as all the new Ph.D.'s roll into the market. A new plateau of compensation may be reached in the 1970's.

In addition to the great expansion of individual institutions of higher learning, there will be an increasing tendency for university centers to cooperate and even coalesce for added strength, particularly in their graduate and research programs. Allan Nevins has put it this way: "Observers of higher education can now foresee the inexorable emergence of an entirely new landscape. It will no longer show us a nation dotted by high academic peaks with lesser hills between; it will be a landscape dominated by mountain ranges." The highest peaks of the future will rise from the highest plateaus.

One such plateau runs from Boston to Washington. At the universities and laboratories situated along this range are found 46 per cent of the American Nobel Prize winners in the sciences and 40 per cent of the members of the National Academy of Sciences. A second range with its peaks runs along the California coast. C. P. Snow has written:

> And now the scientific achievement of the United States is moving at a rate we all ought to marvel at. Think of the astonishing constellation of talent, particularly in the physical sciences, all down the California coast, from Berkeley and Stanford to Pasadena and Los Angeles. There is nothing like that concentration of talent anywhere in the world. It sometimes surprises Europeans to realize how much of the pure science of the entire West is being carried out in the United States. Curiously enough, it often surprises Americans too. At a guess, the figure is something like 80 per cent, and might easily be higher.

The California mountain range has 36 per cent of the Nobel laureates in science and 20 per cent of the members of the National Academy of Sciences. [In the Middle West] the Big Ten and Chicago constitute a third range of academic peaks, with 10 per cent of the Nobel laureates and 14 per cent of the members of the National Academy of Sciences. These three groupings of universities—the East Coast, California, and the Big Ten and Chicago—currently produce over three quarters of the doctorates conferred in the United States. Another range may be in the process of development in the Texas-Louisiana area.

This concentration of talent partly follows history—the location of the older private and public universities. Partly it follows industrial strengths and population centers. But it also has its own logic. No one university can cover all specialties, or cover them well enough so that there is a sufficient cluster of close intellectual colleagues. The scholar dislikes intellectual isolation, and good scholars tend to swarm together. These swarms are extraordinarily productive environments. No library can be complete, nor any graduate curriculum. Some laboratories, to be well used, must be used by more than one university. Thus the Big Ten and Chicago, through their Committee on Institutional Cooperation, are merging their library resources, creating a "common market" for graduate students, diversifying their research laboratories on a common-use basis, and parceling out foreign language specializations. Something similar is happening in the University of California system, and between Berkeley and Stanford. Harvard and M.I.T., Princeton and Pennsylvania, among others, run joint research enterprises. These clustering universities in turn have clustering around them scientifically oriented industrial and governmental enterprises. To match the drawing power of the great metropolis, there now arrives the Ideopolis. The isolated mountain can no longer dominate the landscape; the constellation is greater than the single star and adds to the brightness of the sky.

The rate of growth being forced upon American universities and colleges by the surging enrollment wave will present difficult problems. As President Johnson said in his 1964 Commencement address at the University of Michigan: "More classrooms and more teachers are not enough. We must seek an educational system which grows in excellence as it grows in size." A period of rapid growth is necessarily a period of both flexibility and ingenuity. Institutions can readily adopt on new campuses ideas and programs that would require costly reorganization on older campuses. The University of California, for example, is building its new Santa Cruz campus as a series of small residential colleges, each with its own subject field orientation. The University's new Irvine campus will explore ways of involving organized research units in the formal process of instruction. The new San Diego campus of the university will subdivide its ultimate enrollment of 27,500 students into a series of smaller colleges, with groups of four such colleges constituting largely self-contained sub-campuses of varying academic emphases. The University of the Pacific, in Stockton, California, has established a new residential college in which the entire curriculum is conducted in Spanish. Thus the enrollment explosion may bring unusual opportunities for colleges and universities, along with the heavy burden of numbers.

The current surge in higher education is not, of course, unique to the United States. In Canada the proportion of eighteen- to twenty-one-year-olds in higher education is expected to double in the decade from 1962 to 1972. In France the total enrollment in higher education is expected to soar from around 200,000 now to 500,000 by 1970. In Britain, the much-discussed Robbins Committee Report recommends doubling the number of universities by 1980. These figures reflect the rapidly growing pressures resulting from a vast increase in secondary enrollments throughout much of the world. The decade of the 1950's has seen a world increase of 81 per cent in secondary enrollments and an increase of 71 per cent in college enrollments.

The data both from this country and abroad clearly indicate that we are witnessing everywhere the demise of two long-held notions: that higher education ought to be restricted to a small elite minority, and that only a small percentage of a country's population is capable of benefiting from some kind of higher education. Growth is having quite uneven impacts on American universities. Some, and they are almost always private, are building walls around themselves as aristocratic enclaves protected from the swirling currents of the population explosion. Others, and they are mostly public, are engulfed with more than their share of accommodation to the new hordes, that do not wish to be barbarous, advancing through their gates. The aristocratic enclave offers refuge to the faculty member who wishes protection from the new invasion, and many do; but it will become a more and more isolated element within the society of the future. The university with the open door will suffer the pangs of adjustment, but it will become in the process a more central element in a dynamic society. The one will be a pleasant place to be but increasingly out of tune with the surrounding society. The other will be a less pleasant place to live but will provide a more challenging and exciting environment, and will be more a part of the evolving life around it. Each will have its place, but the places they occupy will grow farther and farther apart.

Shifting Academic Emphases

A second major factor in the changing scene for American higher education is that knowledge is exploding along with population. There is also an explosion in the need for certain skills. The university is responding to all these explosions.

The vastly increased needs for engineers, scientists, and physicians will draw great resources to these areas of the university. Also, some new professions are being born. Others are becoming more formally professional, for example, business administration and social work. The university becomes the chief port of entry for these professions. . . . The life of the universities for a thousand years has been tied into the recognized professions in the surrounding society, and the universities will continue to respond as new professions arise.

The fastest-growing intellectual field today is biology. Here there is a veritable revolution where the doctrine of evolution once reigned supreme. To the classifying efforts of the past are being added the new analytical methods of the present, often drawn from chemistry and physics. There are levels of complexity to be explored in all living structures. The "code of life" can now be read; soon it will be understood, and soon after that, used. It is an intellectual discovery of unique and staggering proportions. The secrets of the atom, much as they have changed and are changing human activity on this planet, may hold no greater significance than the secrets still hidden in the genetic code. If the first half of the twentieth century may be said to have belonged to the physical sciences, the second half may well belong to the biological. Resources within the universities will be poured into the new biology and into the resulting new medicine and agriculture, well supported though medicine and agriculture already are. Medical education and research may be, in particular, on the threshold of revolutionary change.

Another field ready to bloom is that of the creative arts, hitherto the ugly duckling or Cinderella of the academic world. America is bursting with creativity in painting, music, literature, and theater, with a vigor equaled in few other parts of the world today. Italy, France, Spain, Germany, Russia, England, the Low Countries have had great periods of cultural flowering. America is having one now. In the arts the universities have been more hospitable to the historian and the critic than to the creator; the latter has found his havens elsewhere. Yet it is the creativity of science that has given the sciences their prestige in the university. Perhaps creativity will do the same again for the humanities, though there may be less new to create than has recently been true in science, and though the tests of value are far less precise. A very important role remains for the historian of past ages of creativity and for the critic of the current productions. But the universities need to find ways also to accommodate pure creative effort if they are to have places on stage as well as in the wings and in the audience in the great drama of cultural growth now playing on the American stage.

These possibilities for expansion—in the training of engineers, scientists, physicians, and the newer professionals, in biology, and in the creative arts, among various others—raise the problem of balance. As James Bryant Conant has noted, the Western world has had for a thousand years a continuing problem of "keeping a balance between the advancement of knowledge, professional education, general education, and the demands of student life."

But the balance is always changing; this is the unbalancing reality. The balance is not equal treatment, the provision of equal time in some mechanical and eternal way between teaching and research, or between the humanities and science. . . . The essence of balance is to match support with the intellectual creativity of subject fields; with the need for skills of the highest level; with the kinds of expert service that society currently most requires. None of these measures is constant. Balance requires, therefore, a shifting set of judgments which relates facilities and attention to the possibilities inherent in each field, each skill, each activity at that moment of time in that environment, yet preserves for all fields their essential integrity. . . .

Involvement in the Life of Society

The third great change affecting the contemporary university is its thoroughgoing involvement in the nation's daily life. At the heart of this involvement is the growth of the "knowledge industry," which is coming to permeate government and business and to draw into it more and more people raised to higher and higher levels of skill. The production, distribution, and consumption of "knowledge" in all its forms is said to account for 29 per cent of the gross national product, according to Fritz Machlup's calculations; and "knowledge production" is growing at about twice the rate of the rest of the economy. Knowledge has certainly never in history been so central to the conduct of an entire society. What the railroads did for the second half of the last century and the automobile for the first half of this century may be done for the second half of this century by the knowledge industry: that is, to serve as the focal point for national growth. And the university is at the center of the knowledge process.

So the campus and society are undergoing a somewhat reluctant and cautious merger, already well advanced in some fields. M.I.T. is at least as closely related to industry and government as Iowa State ever was to agriculture. Indeed, universities have become "bait" to be dangled in front of industry, with drawing power greater than low taxes or cheap labor. Route 128 around Boston and the great developing industrial complexes in the San Francisco Bay area and southern California reflect the universities in these areas. The Gilpatric report for the Department of Defense explained that 41 per cent of defense contracts for research in the fiscal year 1961 were concentrated in California, 12 per cent in New York, and 6 per cent in Massachusetts, for a total of nearly 60 per cent, in part because these were also "centers of learning." Sterling Forest outside New York City seeks to attract industry by location next to a new university campus. In California, new industrial laboratories were located next to two new university campuses before the first building was built on either of these campuses. Sometimes industry will reach into a university laboratory to extract the newest ideas almost before they are born. Instead of waiting outside the gates, agents are working the corridors. They also work the placement offices. And the university, in turn, reaches into industry, as through the Stanford Research Institute.

The university and segments of industry are becoming more alike. As the university becomes tied into the world of work, the professor—at least in the natural and some of the social sciences—takes on the characteristics of an entrepreneur. Industry, with its scientists and technicians, learns an uncomfortable bit about academic freedom and the handling of intellectual personnel. The two worlds are merging physically and psychologically.

The rapid production of new knowledge has given new significance to university extension slogans about "life-long learning." Television makes it possible for extension to reach into literally every home; the boundaries of the university are stretched to embrace all of society. The student becomes alumnus and the alumnus continues as student; the graduate enters the outside world and the public enters the classroom and the laboratory. Knowledge has the terrifying potential of becoming popular, opening a Pandora's box.

Extension divisions are proving to be increasingly effective administrative devices for linking campus and community in the further pursuit of knowledge. Freer of traditions and rules than regular university academic departments, extension units can respond quickly and in a variety of patterns to meet society's needs for current information and training. Professional schools and colleges, in particular, are making widespread use of extension programs for "refresher" and "continuing education" courses for the active practitioners in their fields. University of California Extension, for example, now enrolls in its courses one of every three lawyers and one of every six physicians in the state. Its total enrollment now numbers some 200,000 students, and it sponsors a remarkably wide range of academic activities including workshops, resident seminars and conferences, theater groups, symposia attracting participants of world renown, and even, recently, a notable scientific expedition to the Galapagos Islands. During the summer of 1964, in response to the growing concern with problems of school integration, University Extension was able to present several short-term workshops and courses on this urgent subject. The new role for knowledge is bringing a new and potentially quite exciting role for extension divisions in American higher education.

The campus becomes a center for cultural life; it has a ready-made audience in its students and faculty and it has the physical facilities. Persons attracted by the performing and visual arts and the lectures come to live around the campus—also assorted crackpots. As the downtown area in some cities decays, the campus takes its place as the cultural center of the community. A new dimension has been added to the land grant idea of service.

The New Deal took professors to Washington from many campuses, the New Frontier from more than just one. In Wisconsin before World War I, the campus and the state house in Madison were exceptionally close. Today the campus is being drawn to the city hall and the state capitol as never before. The politicians need new ideas to meet the new problems; the agencies need expert advice on how to handle the old. The professor can supply both. Keynes concluded his *General Theory* as follows:

> The ideas of economists and political philosophers, both when they are right and when they are wrong, are more powerful than is commonly understood. Indeed the world is ruled by little else. Practical men, who believe themselves to be quite exempt from any intellectual influences, are usually the slaves of some defunct economist. Madmen in authority, who hear voices in the air, are distilling their frenzy from some academic scribbler of a few years back. I am sure that the power of vested interests is vastly exaggerated compared with the gradual encroachment of ideas.

As, for example, the ideas of Keynes.

The university must range itself on the side of intelligent solutions to sometimes unintelligent questions. These questions more and more arise from abroad as well as at home; and the quality of the answers has been made all the more crucial in a world swept by Communist and nationalist revolutions.

There are those who fear the further involvement of the university in the life of society. They fear that the university will lose its objectivity and its freedom. But society is more desirous of objectivity and more tolerant of freedom than it used to be. The university can be further ahead of the times and further to the right of the public—and still keep its equilibrium—than was ever the case before, although problems in this regard are not yet entirely unknown. There are those who fear that the university will be drawn too far from basic to applied research and from applied research to application itself. But the lines dividing these never have been entirely clear, and much new knowledge has been generated at the borders of basic and applied research, and even of applied knowledge and its application. Whitehead once wrote of the creative margin when the "adventure of thought" met "the adventure of action."

Involvement with the Federal Government

Growth and shifting emphases and involvement in society all take money; and which universities get it in the largest quantities will help determine which of them excel a decade or two hence.

Will Federal support be spent according to merit or according to political power? Will private donors continue to do as well as they recently have done for those universities that have done well already? Will the states find new sources of revenue or will their expenditures be held under a lid of no new taxes? The answers to these questions will help predict the standings on the next rating scale of universities.

Of key importance to American universities is the role of the Federal Government, particularly through Federal support of scientific research. This support, which received its great impetus during and after World War II, has already changed the face of the leading American universities almost as much as did the land grant program a century earlier. Federal support has today become a major factor in the total performance of many universities, and the sums involved are substantial. Higher education in 1960 received about $1.5 billion from the Federal Government—a hundredfold increase in twenty years. About one third of this $1.5 billion was for university-affiliated research centers; about one third for project research within universities; and about one third for other things, such as residence hall loans, scholarships, and teaching programs. This last third was expended at colleges as well as universities, but the first two thirds almost exclusively at universities, and at relatively few of them.

The $1 billion for research, though only 10 per cent of total Federal support for research and development, accounted for 75 per cent of all university expenditures on research and 15 per cent of total university budgets. Clearly the shape and nature of university research are profoundly affected by Federal monies. The effects of this extensive Federal aid and the new problems that have arisen as a consequence are many and varied, but the more important of them might be grouped under the two general headings of "Federal influence" and "balance."

1. Federal control as a substantive issue is, as Sidney Hook has said, a "red herring." With a few exceptions—the generally necessary exception of secrecy in certain types of work, and the unnecessary exception of the disclaimer affidavit once required by the National Defense Education Act—there has been no control

in any deleterious sense. The real problem is not one of Federal control but of Federal influence. A Federal agency offers a project. A university need not accept—but, as a practical matter, it usually does. Out of this reality have followed many of the consequences of Federal aid for the universities; and they have been substantial. That they are subtle, slowly cumulative and gentlemanly makes them all the more potent.

A university's control over its own destiny has thus been substantially reduced. University funds from tuition and fees, gifts and endowments, and state sources go through the usual budget-making procedures and their assignment is subject to review in accordance with internal policy. Federal research funds, however, are usually negotiated by the individual scholar with the particular agency, and so bypass the usual review process. Thus 20 to 50 to 80 per cent of a university's expenditures may be handled outside the normal channels. These funds in turn commit some of the university's own funds; they influence the assignment of space; they determine the distribution of time between teaching and research; to a large extent they establish the areas in which the university grows the fastest. Almost imperceptibly, a university is changed.

The authority of the department chairman, the dean, the president is thereby reduced; so also is the role of faculty government. This may have its advantages. The university's internal process of distributing funds would be generally less selective and less flexible than the Federal research project approach. Within a university, the tendency is to give each faculty member about the same opportunity and once having given it to keep giving it thereafter; but the project method allows more attention to exceptional merit and has the advantage that all projects may end some time. Additionally, Federal agencies are more responsive to particular national needs than the universities would be, given the same amount of money to spend according to their own priority system.

There are, however, clearly detrimental effects. Some faculty members come to use the pressure of their agency contacts against their university. They may try to force the establishment of a new administrative unit or the assignment of land for their own special building, in defiance of general university policy or priorities. These pressures, of course, should be withstood; they speak well neither of the professor nor of the agency. Also, some faculty members tend to shift their identification and loyalty from their university to the agency in Washington. The agency becomes the new alma mater. There are especially acute problems when the agency insists on the tie-in sale (if we do this for you, then you must do that for us) or when it requires frequent and detailed progress reports. Then the university really is less than a free agent. It all becomes a kind of "putting-out" system with the agency taking the place of the merchant-capitalist of old.

2. The question of "balance" in Federal aid arises in relation both to support of specific fields within an institution and to distribution of support among institutions of higher learning. Among the totality of university functions, Federal support has been heavily concentrated on research and on graduate and postdoctoral training in fields of national interest. Expenditures have been largely restricted to the physical and biomedical sciences, and to engineering, with only about 3 per cent for the social sciences and hardly any support for the humanities.

All this is said to have destroyed the "balance" among fields, and it is generally concluded that something should be done about it. The balance among fields, however, has never been a static thing. If it were, philosophy, theology, and the classics would still be the dominant areas of study, as they have not been for a long time. Assuming that the balance of 1942, say, was appropriate for 1942, this does not mean it would have been appropriate for 1962. It is not enough to say that the old "balance" has been destroyed. The real question is what should be the proper balance today. It is clear that the flowering of the Renaissance should have affected the "balance" in the sixteenth century. It would seem likely that the splitting of the atom and the deciphering of the genetic code should in their turn affect the balance of the twentieth century. We should expect the most money and the brightest students and the greatest prestige to follow the most exciting new ideas. By and large they have done so, and this is one way of defining the nature of balance.

The real question, it seems to me, is not one of balance in any historical or monetary sense, but rather what is most appropriate to each field in each period. "All fields are equal, only some are more equal than others." There should be no effort to do the same things in the same amounts for each field. Each should receive support in accordance with its current potentialities, and potentialities vary. There are no timeless priorities.

Federal research expenditures have also been heavily focused on relatively few institutions. If both project research and large research centers are included, six universities received 57 per cent of the funds in a recent fiscal year, and twenty universities received 79 per cent. If project research alone is considered, the figures are 28 and 54 per cent. As a percentage of total university expenditures for all purposes among the leading twenty recipients, Federal funds have amounted to 20 to 50 per cent when project research alone is counted, and from 20 to over 80 per cent when the research centers are added. These twenty universities are only about one tenth of all universities in the United States. They constitute the primary "Federal grant" universities.

The project approach almost automatically led to concentration of Federal research effort in a relatively few universities. The universities best equipped to undertake the research were also those with the faculty and facilities to provide for the training of Ph.D.'s. It is no coincidence that the six universities with a little more than 25 per cent of project funds graduated about 25 per cent of the Ph.D.'s; and a similar situation prevails for the top twenty universities. If "only the best will do," this concentration of effort is inevitable. A different result would have been quite surprising.

The concentration of effort has undoubtedly strengthened the facilities and improved the quality of faculties of universities already in the front rank. It has probably widened the gap between those of the first and those of the second and third ranks. It may, in fact, have actually injured universities of the second and third ranks and some colleges by turning their potential faculty members into research personnel in the front-rank universities. The good are better; the poor may well be worse. And it has greatly accentuated the differences between colleges and universities.

The general policy of Federal agencies in allocating research grants to universities for the last two decades has been one of "seeking excellence wherever it is." The period has been one of what I have called "intuitive imbalance." We are now clearly entering a new phase of Federal support policy, one that might be called "bureaucratic balance."

The new balance calls for developing a larger number of outstanding centers of graduate instruction and research. The Seaborg report of 1960 suggested expansion from the present fifteen or twenty centers to thirty or forty over a fifteen-year period. The National Education Improvement Act of 1963 envisaged expansion from twenty to seventy. Teaching is being emphasized along with research. Summer refresher courses for teachers of science, improvement of science textbooks, and language laboratories are programs already established. The National Science Foundation has a large effort under way to improve and renovate equipment for undergraduate teaching in the physical sciences. Undergraduates, as well as graduate students, are being assisted by loans and scholarships. The social sciences are receiving increasing sums of money. More funds are being granted to colleges as well as to universities, and to universities of all ranks.

A particularly significant step in the direction of broadening institutional support is the new science development program announced in the spring of 1964 by the National Science Foundation. This program is specifically designed to raise the over-all quality of science programs in good institutions to the level of excellent. Distinguished institutions are excluded: "Institutions already recognized as being outstanding in science should continue to depend on existing programs for assistance."

Undergraduate as well as graduate institutions will be eligible, and the grants (up to $5 million per institution) may be used in any way the institution chooses to strengthen single departments or related departments, to create new departments, or to improve the entire science program. *Science* magazine, commenting on the NSF plan, said, "it is probably safe to say that the success or failure of this program is going to have a far-reaching influence on the evolution of higher education in the United States."

The approach to a university "as an institution" has interesting implications. If additional universities are to be selected to become centers of strength in research and graduate instruction, then it will be necessary for the Federal Government to be concerned with the "general health of the institution." This will be a notable departure from historical practice, except in agriculture. If we are to move toward Federal orientation to the "total function of the university," then the University Grants Committee in Great Britain is the outstanding precedent, and one that has received some support in the United States. However, there are only about thirty universities in Great Britain, and it is clear what is and what is not a university. Additionally, the University Grants Committee has come to exercise more influence over the establishment of new programs, the cost and size and even the appearance of new buildings, the equalization of faculty salaries among institutions, and the determination of admission policies than would currently be acceptable if it came from the Federal Government in this country.

Some hard choices must be faced. The decentralized project approach of the last two decades has much to recommend it. It is selective on merit, flexible in accordance with quality of performance, and responsive to national goals. The universities and their scholars retain substantial freedom. But such dominant reliance on the project approach is no longer likely. It is said that support to institutions as such will "give a university the necessary autonomy" and will permit dispersion of effort and better balance in several directions. It is difficult, however, to assess the merit of a total institution as complex as a modern university. One alternative is to rely on a formula, as in the case of agriculture in the land-grant institutions. Another is to be guided by political influence; and this is increasingly happening. Interuniversity competition is being taken from the quasi-academic arena of the agency committee to the legislative halls.

The partnership of the Federal Government with higher education and particularly with the Federal grant universities over the last two decades has been enormously productive in enlarging the pool of scientific ideas and skills. Now we are entering a new phase of widening and deepening relationships. This new phase can carry the American commitment to education to new heights of endeavor. It can also preserve the traditional freedom of higher education from excessive control. It can enlarge the horizons of equality of opportunity. It can maintain and even increase the margin for excellence. The challenge is to make certain it does all these things. [For another critical appraisal of the Federal role in higher education, see "Serving Knowledge—Or the Government?" in Section II, below.]

However this turns out, the scene of American higher education will continue to be marked by great variety, and this is one of its great strengths. The large and the small, the private and the public, the general and the specialized—all add their share to over-all excellence. The total system is extraordinarily flexible, decentralized, competitive—and productive. The new can be tried, the old tested with considerable skill and alacrity. Pluralism in higher education matches the pluralistic American society. The general test of higher education is not how much is done poorly, and some is; rather it is how much is done superbly, and a great deal is, to the nation's great benefit.

Changes Still to Come

But there are some problems still to be fully faced; and they are problems of consequence.

1. One is the improvement of undergraduate instruction in the university. The much-advertised conflict between teaching and research puts the problem the wrong way. The teaching of graduate students is so closely tied to research that if research is improved, graduate instruction is almost bound to be improved also. And the almost universal experience seems to be that Federal research support has improved graduate instruction. At the undergraduate level, however, a "subtle discounting of the teaching process" has been aided and abetted. [For further discussion of this problem, see Section IV of this book, *The Faculty: Pressures and Problems.*]

The reasons for the general deterioration of undergraduate teaching are several. Teaching loads and student contact hours have been reduced. Faculty members are more frequently on leave or temporarily away from the campus; some are never more than temporarily on campus. More of the instruction falls to teachers who are not members of the regular faculty. The best graduate students prefer fellowships and research assistantships to teaching assistantships. Postdoctoral fellows who might fill the gap usually do not teach. Average class size has been increasing.

There seems to be a "point of no return" after which research, consulting, graduate instruction become so absorbing that faculty efforts can no longer be concentrated on undergraduate instruction as they once were. This process has been going on for a long time; Federal research funds have intensified it. As a consequence, undergraduate education in the large university is more likely to be acceptable than outstanding; educational policy from the undergraduate point of view is largely neglected.

Improvement of undergraduate instruction will require the solution of many sub-problems: how to give adequate recognition to the teaching skill as well as to the research performance of the faculty; how to create a curriculum that serves the needs of the student as well as the research interests of the teacher; how to prepare the generalist as well as the specialist in an age of specialization looking for better generalizations; how to treat the individual student as a unique human being in the mass student body; how to make the university seem smaller even as it grows larger; how to establish a range of contact between faculty and students broader than the one-way route across the lectern or through the television screen; how to raise educational policy again to the forefront of faculty concerns.

2. Another major task is to create a more unified intellectual world. We need to make contact between the two, the three, the many cultures; to open channels of intelligent conversation across the disciplines and divisions; to close the gap between C. P. Snow's "Luddites" and scientists; to answer fragmentation with general theories and sensitivities. Even philosophy, which once was the hub of the intellectual universe, is now itself fragmented into such diverse specialities as mathematics and semantics. However, the physical sciences are drawing together as new discoveries create more basic general theories; the biological sciences may be pulled together in the process now going on; the social sciences might be unified around the study of organizations and the relations of individuals to and within them. Biochemistry and social psychology

may come to be central focalizing fields. As knowledge is drawn together, if in fact it is, a faculty may again become a community of masters; but "a sense of the unity . . . of all knowledge" is still a very long way off.

3. A third problem is to relate administration more directly to individual faculty and students in the massive institution. We need to decentralize below the campus level to the operating agencies; to make the collective faculty a more vital, dynamic, progressive force as it now is only at the departmental level; to bridge the growing chasm between the department that does the teaching and the institute that does the research, with the faculty member torn between; to make the old departments and divisions more compatible with the new divisions of knowledge; to make it possible for an institution to see itself in totality rather than just piecemeal and in the sweep of history rather than just at a moment of time; to bring an understanding of both internal and external realities to all those intimately related to the process, so that there may be greater understanding; to see to it that administration serves and stimulates rather than rules the institution, that it is expendable when necessary and flexible all the time; to assure that the university can do better what it does best; to solve the whole range of governmental problems within the university.

4. Additionally, there is the urgent issue of how to preserve a margin for excellence in a populist society, when more and more of the money is being spent on behalf of all of the people. The great university is of necessity elitist—the elite of merit—but it operates in an environment dedicated to an egalitarian philosophy. How may the contribution of the elite be made clear to the egalitarians, and how may an aristocracy of intellect justify itself to a democracy of all men? It was equality of opportunity, not equality *per se,* that animated the founding fathers and the progress of the American system; but the forces of populist equality have never been silent, the battle between Jeffersonianism and Jacksonianism never finally settled.

George Beadle, president of the University of Chicago, once implied that the very large American university (but not his own) might be like the dinosaur which "became extinct because he grew larger and larger and then sacrificed the evolutionary flexibility he needed to meet changing conditions"; its body became too large for its brain. David Riesman has said that the leading American universities are "directionless . . . as far as major innovations are concerned"; they have run out of foreign models to imitate; they have lost their "ferment." The fact is that they are not directionless; they have been moving in clear directions and with considerable speed. These directions, however, have not been set as much by the university's visions of its destiny as by the external environment, including the Federal Government, the foundations, the surrounding and sometimes engulfing industry.

But the really new problems of today and tomorrow may lend themselves less to solutions by external authority; they may be inherently problems for internal resolution. And these solutions, if they are to come, are more likely to emerge on the campuses of those old, private universities which have prided themselves on control of their own destiny, and on the totally new campuses of the state universities in America (and the new public universities in Britain). The university for the twenty-first century is more likely to emerge from these environments than from any others. Out of the pride of the old and the vacuum of the new may come the means to make undergraduate life more exciting, intellectual discourse more meaningful, administration more human. And perhaps there will arise a more dynamic demonstration of how excellence makes democracy more vital and its survival more assured. Then the contemporary American university may indeed rise to "the heights of the times." Then it may demonstrate that it has a mind as well as a body.

II. SOME ASPECTS OF THE CURRENT CRISIS

EDITOR'S INTRODUCTION

Few events in recent academic history have stirred such widespread interest and comment as those which took place on the Berkeley campus of the University of California during the winter of 1964-1965. For many, the so-called Berkeley crisis symbolized the crisis besetting American higher education as a whole—students lost in a shuffle of IBM cards, professors locked inaccessibly away in their laboratories, administrators quietly eliminating whatever might be left of the "community of scholars" atmosphere on campus. In this increasingly bureaucratic setting, with its impersonal rules and regulations, students chose to revolt on the issue of free speech. But their real complaint, in the eyes of many observers, went far deeper.

The events at Berkeley focused national attention on these deep-seated grievances and called forth lively debate on the nature of the crisis in higher education and what should be done about it. Were students merely letting off steam in a new, political direction? Were their protests prompted by the rapid changes taking place on campus, or were they a signal that changes are not being made fast enough? These and other questions could be asked of campuses all across the country. With costs rising, are students being short-changed on their investment in college? Is quantity education replacing quality education and threatening to turn our institutions of higher learning into "diploma mills"?

This section examines more closely some of the critical problems confronting higher education in the wake of the transformation that is taking place. Each of the first four articles deals with a separate problem area. A political scientist at Cornell University, Andrew Hacker, explores the quantity-quality dilemma and concludes that in some respects students have much of substance to complain about. Next, the editors of *U. S. News & World Report* describe the troubles afflicting state universities, especially their struggle to cope with rising enrollments. The third article focuses attention on a problem of great concern to young people and their parents everywhere: the mounting costs of a college degree. And the fourth article describes the concern arising over increased Federal influence on the aims and content of higher education.

The last article in this section is given over to a rather lengthy analysis of what happened at Berkeley and why. Two political scientists on the scene express general sympathy with the student cause and explain why the Berkeley "rebels" had a right to feel angry. Their view of events, though sharply disputed by many commentators who took a less sympathetic attitude toward the Berkeley Free Speech Movement, nonetheless draws into focus the uneasy atmosphere that prevailed at a leading "multiversity." As California President Clark Kerr himself noted, the students were "restless." In the ultimate expression of their restlessness, most observers would agree, the important question to be analyzed is not How? but Why?

THE "QUALITY-QUANTITY" CRISIS [1]

Hardly a commencement or baccalaureate address this week will not contain at least one allusion, however veiled, to the fact that this [1965] was the Year of the Demonstration. If some campus protests have been political while others have exemplified educational discontents, it remains to say that students at schools as widely contrasted as Berkeley, St. John's and Yale have rallied, marched, signed and sat in displays of vehemence and in numbers not equaled in this generation.

A major reason for these stirrings is that not a few American undergraduates have become convinced that they are being short-changed. Feeling cheated on the educational end, especially at the larger institutions, they are ripe for any demonstration against authority in general and campus officialdom in particular. Nevertheless, it must be recorded that the protests over the quality of higher education are foredoomed to failure. They are outcries

[1] From "The College Grad Has Been Short-Changed," by Andrew Hacker, a member of the Department of Government, Cornell University. New York *Times Magazine.* p 25+. Je. 6, '65. Copyright © 1965 by The New York Times Company. Reprinted by permission.

against conditions which will become even further entrenched
in the years to come.

What is distressing is that so many students, faculty members
and observers of the educational scene still think that serious reforms are possible. For this reason the facts of modern university
life deserve to be catalogued, if only because so many of us will
have to live with them.

The Upsurge in Numbers

In the first place, colleges and universities will become larger,
and consequently more bureaucratic and impersonal. Within a
generation, only a minor fraction of the student population will
be attending small, independent colleges. Already six out of every
ten students are in institutions having enrollments of over 5,000,
whereas a dozen years ago, less than half were in schools of that
size.

The reason for this is not that small colleges are going out of
business—hardly any do—but that most of them are becoming
larger. This is especially the case with publicly supported institutions. Whereas every state used to have its network of normal and
A.&M. schools, these are now being transformed into universities
with no ceilings foreseen for their enrollments. What was once
a teachers' college in Carbondale is now Southern Illinois University, with over 17,000 students. Plans are being made to expand
New York's old normal schools—like Brockport, Fredonia, Geneseo,
New Paltz, Oneonta, Potsdam—so they can absorb the tens of
thousands of students in search of a college education. And except
for a handful of Amhersts and Swarthmores, virtually all of the
small private colleges are anxious to raise their enrollments, sometimes for financial reasons but also for purposes of prestige.

It is easy to give publicity to projects and experiments intended
to counter this trend. About ten years ago, for example, California
declared that it would make its Riverside campus the "Amherst"
of the system, with an enrollment limited to about 1,000 liberal arts
majors. As of now, Riverside has grown to some 3,000 and its
plans are to have as many as 14,000 students on the campus by

1980, many of them working for advanced degrees. So much for the "Amherst" idea.

Now we are hearing about the new Santa Cruz campus, this time to be the "Oxford" of the Coast, having a series of small colleges, each with its own professors giving tutorials, on a prominence above the Pacific. It is impossible to see how such an educational luxury can survive, especially in a state with so many teen-agers knocking on college doors. The Santa Cruz plan, like Riverside's before it, is expensive in fact and undemocratic in theory. These are two powerful strikes against intimate education, public or private.

Larger enrollments mean larger classes. In a small school, only 15 students would elect medieval history and a professor would be assigned to teach them. In a large place, 150 sign up for such a course—and the professor lectures to them en masse. (Why not have 10 professors, each teaching a class of 15? The answer, apart from the fact that no department has 10 medievalists, is that such an arrangement is outrageously expensive. That is why colleges are expanding their enrollments to begin with.) One result is that students will come to know fewer and fewer professors on a personal basis. But if they will have less to do with the faculty, they are destined for many more encounters with the administration.

The Rising Bureaucracy

On every campus, students find they must spend more and more time dealing with an expanding bureaucracy. Regular visits must be paid to administrative purlieus to fill in forms in triplicate, to be photographed in duplicate (face and lungs), to appeal, to petition, to ask permission. They must not fold, mutilate, staple or spindle the IBM cards representing their studenthood; they must secure prior approval for all manner of social, political and domestic arrangements if they are to ensure that their existence does not violate the rules contained in the thick handbooks of codes and regulations. (One might ask if this is not the case in every sphere of modern organized life. The answer is that a university is supposed to be a realm of scholars, a community of ideas and hence to be spared such encumbrances.)

The ranks of the administrators have been expanding much faster than those of the teaching faculty and this trend will doubtless continue. I have yet to learn of a single college or university where the growth rate of its administrative corps is less than that of the professoriat. Educational administrators, like their counterparts elsewhere, are adept at discovering new services they can perform, new committees they can create, new reports they can write.

They have an advantage over the professors in this respect, for they possess both the will and the skill for arrogating new powers and functions to themselves. And they have, after all, a sweet reasonableness on their side. Would anyone care to suggest that a college could operate without registrars, controllers, deans of men, housemothers, public-relations emissaries, guidance counselors, activities advisers, residence managers, proctors, pastors, research coordinators, placement officers, clinic technicians and development directors?

Every day these officials find new ways to intrude their presence into student life. It may well be that undergraduates are looked after better than ever before: they are ministered with food and housing, counseling and recreation, medicine and religion, career guidance and financial assistance. Yet if undergraduates are driven into the arms of the burgeoning bureaucracies, this is partly because the professors are so seldom at home.

Hard-Pressed Professors

Much has been written and said about the retreat from the classroom, about the increasing unwillingness of professors to teach or otherwise to meet with students. No elaboration is needed here, except to say that the charges are true. This is the age of the foundation grant, of prolonged academic travel, of frequent leaves. It is also the era of conferences, workshops and symposia that draw professors (all expenses paid) away from the campus, frequently in the middle of classes. The mere murmuring of the sacred incantation "research" is sufficient excuse to bow out of introductory courses, to confine one's offerings to graduate seminars, to depart for another institution where more grandiose projects will be more generously underwritten.

But the focus here is on the future of higher education and it is relevant to consider the rising generation of professors. These young men are being suitably indoctrinated even while in graduate school. For one thing, they learn the dominant fashions in their disciplines and commit themselves intellectually (if that is the word) to the going trends. This is especially necessary for the less talented (in other words the majority) for the rising tide of fashion offers the safest haven for mediocre minds. . . .

Most of the new professors like to think of themselves primarily as scholars, and this attitude is held even by those incapable of making more than a quite minimal contribution to human knowledge. This being the case, who is going to do the teaching? This question would be a pressing one even if the every-man-a-researcher fetish did not exist.

Assuming that one professor is needed for every 10 students, for every million undergraduates we add to our college rolls—and we are currently adding a million every three years—100,000 more teachers will be needed. Yet fewer than 15,000 Ph.D.'s are produced annually in this country—and not all of these go into teaching. And of those who do, not all are exactly excited over the prospect of spending their careers in the classroom.

At the same time, there is no indication that reputable colleges or universities are willing to sign up, on a permanent basis, people with lesser degrees. The chasm between the M.A. and the Ph.D. is a yawning one. After all, kindergarten teachers have M.A.'s. The notion that each college will establish a separate "teaching faculty," unencumbered by the publish-or-perish test, is illusory. The Ph.D. standard has been set, and nowadays even independent undergraduate schools find themselves going through the motions of expecting research and publication from their faculty.

The result will be larger classes, more machine-graded examinations and more televised instruction. (The "solution" of less classroom work and more "independent" study is another delusion; it takes a professor far more time to supervise and evaluate the independent work of students than it does to teach them in groups.) It is fruitless to discuss the wisdom of developments such as electronic education. They are going to come, like it or not, and whatever is inevitable ceases to be a worth-while issue for discussion. If 3 million new places are going to be created for students over the coming decade, the 300,000 new professors who will be needed to teach them are nowhere in sight. And those who are recruited will spend less time in actual teaching than ever before.

Do Students Seek Quality?

Does all this really trouble most of today's and tomorrow's students? I suspect that it does not. When all is said and done, the vast majority of American undergraduates are not greatly concerned with the quality of the education they are receiving. The millions of teen-agers filling up our colleges and universities are there for career purposes. They know, better than their parents, that a degree is absolutely necessary for financial and social success; and they are willing to spend four not-too-arduous years to become properly accredited. Most undergraduates have enrolled for eminently practical majors—business and engineering for the boys and education for the girls. Those doing liberal arts subjects are the minority, and very few of these have any illusions that they are engaged in learning for its own sake.

Most of today's students are not intellectuals, nor are they capable of becoming so. They do not object to large, anonymous classes. They have no ideas of their own to put forward and they want to be told what they have to know. Eight out of ten students discover that they have nothing to say at such times as they *do* meet with a real professor at close range. Hence their preference for fraternities and sororities, activities and athletics, and the nonacademic chit-chat with guidance counselors, activity directors and religious advisers.

Once we admit that most young Americans have no genuine interest in or talent for the intellectual life, the problem of quality in education begins to recede. It may even cease to be a problem.

Certainly, this year's protesters and demonstrators were not representative of their classmates, and it is instructive how quickly their ranks have tended to dwindle away after the first flamboyant outbursts. So long as a school will give an undergraduate his passport into the upper-middle-class without demanding more than he can give with fifteen weekly hours of studying, few are going to complain.

Perhaps the root of the trouble lies in the tendency to compare American colleges of today with those of earlier generations or with their European counterparts. At the turn of the century, only 4 per cent of the eighteen-to-twenty-one age group was enrolled in colleges and universities, and even in Europe today only about 10 per cent are in institutions of higher learning.

The United States, in contrast, has committed itself to higher education for almost half of those of college age and the proportion may well rise to 70 per cent. If the consequence is mass production, this is bound to happen when a nation tries to give the best of everything to everyone.

The only possible way to reintroduce quality into higher education would be to deny college places of any sort to three out of four who are now applying. But a democracy cannot tell its citizens—who are, after all, articulate taxpayers and awakened voters—that their children will have to make do with lesser credentials. An aristocratic posture makes sense only when the masses admit to their inferior status and defer to their betters.

When, as in America, the majority is affluent and self-confident, people come to feel entitled to all manner of things that were once the exclusive privileges of a minority. Admission to a college, with the opportunities it opens for ascending careers, can no longer be confined to a small fraction of the population. Having chosen to be a democracy we must accept its consequences.

Colleges and universities as constituted at present have too many contented constituents for them to change their ways. Most of the students, at least half of the professors and all of the educational administrators are faring better than ever before and are experiencing opportunities that only a favored few knew in earlier days. The dissenting members of the academic community are setting themselves against the combined forces of democracy in education and technology in learning. Like many rebels they are nostalgic for a society they never knew and a world they can never know.

STATE UNIVERSITIES IN TROUBLE [2]

A crisis that is going to get worse before it gets better has hit the campuses of state universities all over the United States.

Many people still think their sons and daughters can always go to their state university if turned down by the big-name private schools of their choice.

These people are in for a shock. In state after state, the public universities are being forced to turn away thousands of qualified students. The old rule that every graduate of an accredited high school has the right to enter a state college is being repealed by events.

Because their warnings of impending crisis were largely ignored, educators say, money alone cannot solve the public-college shortage in years just ahead....

Last summer, reported Dr. John W. Lederle, president of the University of Massachusetts,

We had about 12,000 applications for the freshman class.

Ten thousand would have qualified for admission if we had had room. But we had only 2,600 places.

This year we look for 15,000 applicants. We hope to squeeze in 3,800.

New England . . . has been notorious for its failure to support higher education. We tended to export many of our college students to other states, and we depended on our prestigious private schools to take in others.

In Massachusetts, we are now recognizing that we can't export young people who want a college education. There are terrible pressures to take care of our own people.

What we have here now is awfully close to a year-round operation, and we're expanding as fast as humanly possible. It's not just a question of physical expansion. Getting new faculty members is a serious problem. But if we had all the money in the world we couldn't solve this problem by ourselves.

In spite of all our expansion, there are certainly going to be some high school graduates who are not going to have any place to go to college.

[2] From "Now: Crisis for State Universities?" *U. S. News & World Report.* 58:55-60. F. 1, '65. Reprinted from *U. S. News & World Report,* published at Washington.

How Big Should You Get?

President Wilson H. Elkins of the University of Maryland believes that a decision must be made soon on just how large his school is going to become.

There will be about 26,000 students on Maryland's main campus this year, and probably 30,000 by 1966.

The campus could be expanded to accommodate about 50,000, but Mr. Elkins said: "I don't think that would be desirable." Ideally, he would like to hold main campus enrollment to 25,000.

While no one knows what the maximum student enrollment should be, Maryland's president said, a vast expansion would make it extremely difficult "to keep in touch with students."

Maryland is thinking about restricting admissions to freshmen who ranked in the upper half of their high school graduating classes. A decision awaits expansion of other college facilities in the state, because, as Mr. Elkins put it:

"We can't say to a student, 'Go elsewhere,' unless we are sure that there is somewhere else for him to go."

The stated policy of the University of Michigan is to admit all "qualified" high school graduates who are residents of the state.

Vice President Roger Heyns said the university, now operating forty-nine weeks out of every fifty-two, does not intend to change its admission policy. However, the university official added, the admission of about 400 Michigan residents will have to be deferred from September 1965 to January 1966 because there isn't room for them.

Michigan has no hard-and-fast rules on what constitutes a "qualified" student, but resident high school seniors are told by the university that they shouldn't consider applying unless: they finish in the top 25 per cent of their graduating classes, can be highly recommended by their high school principals or counselors, and achieve at least national-average scores in the College Entrance Examination Board tests.

When it comes to out-of-state students, Dr. Heyns said, the university is in "a real bind." He reported that for every 1,000 openings for out-of-state freshmen there are 6,000 applications.

Beginning next autumn, a policy of "controlled growth" will go into effect at the University of Minnesota.

One result, according to T. E. Kellogg, Minnesota's admissions officer, will be that "about 1,500 to 2,000 students who would like to enroll next autumn, and who would have been eligible this year, won't make it."

Enrollment at the University of Minnesota is now about 38,500.

Mr. Kellogg said that, under present plans, "we don't want to get much beyond 42,000."

We still expect steady growth, but we want to control it. . . . Up to now, we were able to accommodate any increase in enrollment.

We were flexible with our facilities and staff, so we could adjust to growth. But we finally reached a point where we have very little flexibility. And, instead of diminishing the quality of education here, the university has decided to match the enrollment with available resources.

As part of the controlled-growth policy, admission standards at Minnesota, already high for a state university, will be raised higher.

Minnesota has not had to defer admissions up to now, Mr. Kellogg said, but some applicants this year may have to be told that they will be considered only if space is available.

An "Unprecedented Increase"

With a jump of 2,890 students last autumn, enrollment at Wayne State University in Detroit reached an all-time high of 25,000.

"This unprecedented increase in students so far outstripped our predictions," said President Clarence B. Hilberry, "that we are forced to ask the state legislature for an emergency appropriation to adequately provide for the overflow."

Enrollment at the University of Texas climbed from 16,000 in 1954 to 24,000 last year.

Nevertheless, university officials say they still have room and do not expect to refuse admission to any qualified student, from inside or outside the state, in 1965.

Higher entrance requirements, however, are expected to cut down the number of Texans seeking admission. These higher requirements become effective in June. . . .

The University of Texas now operates on a two-semester system which fills up nine months of the year. There is also a summer session, divided into two six-week terms. Classes are held six days a week, from 8 A.M. to 6 P.M., during the long session, and five days per week in the summer.

As the demand for higher education increases in Texas, costs continue to climb. Many educators in the state feel that a choice will have to be made soon between higher tuition and higher taxes.

A master plan for higher education, developed several years ago, has given California a head start in efforts to cope with the college crush.

The plan has taken a big load off the University of California —and at the same time made it possible for more than half the people of college age in the state to go to college.

On the seven campuses of the University of California, there are now more than 71,000 students. This includes an 18 per cent increase in one year.

While the university wants to keep on admitting out-of-state students, to give a broader mix to the student body, it has become necessary to reduce the number of these admissions.

Only those in the top 6 per cent of their high school graduating classes will now be admitted from outside California. If further limitation becomes necessary, university officials say, the present $600-a-year tuition will be raised.

Under California's master plan, about 149,000 students are getting their education at 18 state colleges, separate from the University.

Almost 450,000 are packed into California's 75 junior colleges, where they can study for two years and transfer later, if their grades justify it.

Everywhere, there is a crush. San Francisco State typifies the pressure on state colleges in California. It has been operating at

106 per cent of capacity by scheduling classes from 8 A.M. to 10 P.M.

Still it had to turn away 5,000 qualified applicants last autumn. These students had to go knocking on the doors of other state colleges or junior colleges.

Avalanche of Freshmen

Across the nation in 1964, freshman classes averaged 17 per cent more than in 1963.

Another rise of 10 to 20 per cent in freshman applications is likely at state universities in 1965, on the basis of population growth alone.

On top of the present stampede, many educators see a potential new group of students on the horizon, created by President Lyndon Johnson's plans.

As a starter, Mr. Johnson wants to give Federal scholarships to 140,000 needy students a year, and guaranteed loans to thousands of others who cannot afford college without financial aid. [As written into law in 1965, the Federal Higher Education Act provides just that.—Ed.]

The question that college authorities raise: Where, in the next few years, can room be found for these additional thousands of young people?

State universities almost everywhere are deep in plans for expansion. Meanwhile, emergency measures are the rule.

Many schools are going into year-round operation, adopting the trimester—three-term—system or dividing the school year into quarters.

Class days are being lengthened almost universally, and there are Saturday sessions on some campuses.

Three students are being crammed into dormitory rooms built for two. Kitchen spaces are being pressed into use as bedrooms.

Longe-range college expansion programs now under way will be costly.

One estimate is that the United States will have to spend about $75 billion in the next decade to meet college demands. Most of that sum would go for public institutions.

In their search for solutions, probably no two states are following exactly the same plan. In general, however, states are moving on these three fronts:

First, they're setting up entirely new junior colleges, usually in suburbs of major cities, to handle the mass of high school graduates.

These junior colleges offer a chance at higher education to students who didn't do too well in high school. They have an advantage, too, in that most of the students can live at home, reducing costs for both the institution and the student.

Second, states are expanding their networks of "second layer" colleges, which are branches of the state universities or independent state colleges.

Many were once "teachers' colleges." Some of the newer ones are private schools that have been taken over by the states. Typically, these colleges admit higher-ranking students than those in junior colleges.

Third, some states are expanding their main universities. At the same time, they are limiting enrollments to the best students, and emphasizing professional schools and postgraduate work.

There's a tendency to make the main university a more or less "elite" school that is beyond the reach of the majority of high school graduates in the state.

This tendency toward excluding students distresses many educators in the public institutions. Most want to get back to the idea that higher education should be available to all who seek it.

THE PROBLEM OF SOARING COSTS [3]

For 1,425 of the 6,700 high school seniors who have applied to enter Harvard College next fall, there will be good news today [April 19, 1965]. They will go to their mailboxes and learn that they have been accepted by the Cambridge, Massachusetts, institution. But in the homes of many of the successful applicants, joy will not be unalloyed.

[3] From "Paying for College," by Roger Ricklefs, staff reporter. *The Wall Street Journal.* p 1+. Ap. 19, '65. Reprinted by permission.

The explanation: Their fathers will be facing up to the hard fact that even if expenses don't rise at all, sending their boys to Harvard for four years will cost more than $13,000, excluding transportation between home and Cambridge. Tuition alone is now $1,760 a year, up from $800 a decade ago.

Figures such as these are alarming millions of parents with college-bound children. From the 1951-52 academic year to the 1963-64 period, the average annual cost of tuition, fees and room and board at private American colleges increased from $1,103 per student to $2,049, a jump of 86 per cent. Over the same span, the cost of attending state and other public institutions rose from $699 to $1,044 a year for residents, a gain of almost 50 per cent. The climb is certain to continue. The American Council on Education expects tuition at both private and public institutions to increase 50 per cent in the next ten years.

A Complex Affair

Meeting soaring college expenses is taxing the resources and imagination of many American families. Even people who would usually be classed as prosperous are often unable to come up with the cash to pay their offsprings' bills. The upshot is that financing a college education is becoming an increasingly complex affair, with more and more students supplementing family funds with scholarships, loans and income from jobs. As just one indication of this trend, the number of scholarship holders among freshmen at the University of Chicago has jumped from 36 per cent five years ago to 54 per cent now.

The experience of Edward H. Foster, a Columbia University English major who will be graduated this June, shows the variety of resources a student sometimes draws on.

Mr. Foster figures his total bill for the current year at Columbia will exceed $3,400. Tuition of $1,900 is covered by a scholarship. Mr. Foster's mother, a widow who earns $8,000 a year as a school administrator in Williamsburg, Massachusetts, is contributing about $600 toward his expenses. Another $500 comes from savings accumulated by Mr. Foster while working last summer as a country club bartender—a job he succeeded at by referring frequently to a recipe book kept under the bar. During the academic year he is earning more than $400 by doing ten hours of clerical work a week for the English department.

In past years Mr. Foster has also drawn on $1,000 he saved before entering college, as well as on $1,500 borrowed from a loan fund at Columbia. "Nearly everybody I know is using several sources to finance his education the way I am," he comments. "There must be some people whose parents pay for everything, but I don't know any."

More Scholarships

Scholarship opportunities are growing. Some 65 per cent of the 2,700 students at Columbia College—the university's undergraduate liberal arts college for men—receive a total of $1.85 million in scholarship aid each year, up from $350,000 a decade ago. Half the money comes from Columbia itself, and the rest is contributed by outside sources, including New York State and corporations, according to Robert L. Smith, assistant dean in charge of the college's financial aid.

Colleges are keenly aware that rising educational costs necessitate more scholarship aid for students from middle- and upper-income families. One recent survey shows that for every college scholarship holder from a family earning less than $3,000 a year, there are four from families earning over $11,000.

Says Dean Smith of Columbia: "Ten years ago almost nobody with a family income over $13,000 or $14,000 a year could receive a scholarship at Columbia. But today if family expenses are high enough, we grant scholarships to men whose parents earn even $20,000 or $22,000." The Columbia official cites the case of one student who received a $900 scholarship this year even though his parents have an annual income of $22,000. The parents would have been hard-pressed to send the student to Columbia this year because of high family expenses—including outlays for three other children enrolled in private institutions.

Despite the growing availability of funds, colleges still can't afford a scholarship for every needy student. Consequently, more students are turning to loans from their schools and other sources which they pledge to repay after graduation. Loans to Columbia students totaled $398,000 this year, up from $58,000 a decade ago.

Banks' Role Grows

Banks and other financial institutions are also lending money directly to students for college expenses, often under programs in which states or private groups guarantee the loans. Loans under such programs, many of which didn't exist five years ago, should total about $100 million this year, according to Keith G. Cone, senior vice president of Chicago's LaSalle National Bank, who has studied the subject.

The Federal Government also supplies student loan funds. Under the National Defense Education Act, Uncle Sam contributes 90 per cent and the college 10 per cent. Repayment at low 3 per cent interest doesn't begin until a year after the student finishes full-time studies. Students are borrowing some $100 million under the NDEA plan this year; since the program started in 1958 about 600,000 students have taken advantage of it.

With college costs rising and with academic requirements stiffer than ever, few students can put in enough hours on jobs to pay all their expenses, especially at highly competitive private colleges. Some colleges report difficulty filling their low-paying menial jobs; they say students often prefer to borrow money or feel they can't afford the time a job takes. But on many campuses, a large and often growing number of students still earn at least part of their financial needs by working. Increasingly, middle- and upper-income students squeezed by climbing costs are joining the campus work force, educators say. The University of Wisconsin says that well over 20,000 of its 38,000 students hold jobs.

Some institutions have started programs to teach students skills they can use to earn money while in college. Harvard now offers noncredit instruction in such subjects as computer programing and short-order cooking. Columbia started a similar program two years ago. "A man who learns bookkeeping or bartending can earn $2 or $2.50 an hour, compared with $1.35 to $1.50 for unskilled library assistants and messengers," says Alexander Stoia, head of student employment at Columbia.

Job opportunities related to future careers are multiplying. In recent years companies, government agencies and nonprofit organizations have started or expanded summer intern and trainee programs for college students. Last summer, for example, ten Columbia electrical engineering students found such jobs and earned between $346 and $650 a month. Columbia's departmental assistant program, started three years ago, lets students perform routine research and clerical work for professors in their major fields.

But however hard-working students may be, much of the burden of increased college costs inevitably falls on parents. Savings programs and insurance plans begun years earlier, when costs were lower, often prove inadequate when the day of enrollment arrives, and as a result many parents must turn to loans. Mortgage loans are one of the most widely used sources of funds. The American Bankers Association reports that outstanding home mortgage loans for college bills now total well over $1 billion and are rising fast.

SERVING KNOWLEDGE—OR THE GOVERNMENT? [4]

The sheer size of government research and development spending—currently at the $15 billion annual level—is startling. Much more disturbing to many Americans, however, is a rising storm of complaints over government sponsorship of research in universities and what it is doing to educational systems.

Government R&D [Research and Development] money going into college coffers already amounts to $1.2 billion annually. By 1970, the flow, increasing at a rate of 15 per cent to 20 per cent yearly, could cross the $2.5 billion mark.

This trend already is raising ticklish questions like these:

Are college professors being kept from doing their prime job—teaching?

[4] From "Uncle Sam: Big Man on Campus." *Business Week.* p 90-2+. N. 2, '63. Reprinted from the November 2, 1963 issue of *Business Week* by special permission. Copyrighted © 1963 by McGraw-Hill, Inc.

Is this huge flow of money moving into fields that properly deserve research support?

Has Washington really thought through the research process and what its role should be?

And how about dangers of university dependence on these Federal funds? Where is the road leading? Does the nation want such changes?

To get the answers to these and similar questions, *Business Week* reporters visited campuses across the nation and picked up comments from college and university administrators like these:

"Withdrawal of government money for research and development in universities would have a catastrophic effect on education."

"There are imbalances and headaches, of course. But government research money is an indispensable teaching tool in the United States today."

"In essence, the government is supporting us. We don't like some of the problems, such as incessant supervision. But there's no turning back now. . . ."

I. *Haves and Have-nots*

Generally, the survey found schools getting large slices of the cake well satisfied; those receiving crumbs complained. Last year, ten universities divided 38 per cent of the government's research allocations; 20 shared close to 75 per cent or $800 million.

Spokesmen for the University of Illinois, University of Chicago, Stanford, and Columbia—all among the top ten in receipt of government research and development funds this year [1963] —agree that the "bureaucrats have displayed surprisingly good judgment in terms of the research work they are sponsoring at universities."

Says Dr. Frederick E. Terman, vice president and provost of Stanford: "The emphasis is on quality projects. The government shops around for the best institutions."

Government funds at Stanford, he notes, have enabled faculty members to put in more time on research, to carry a lighter teach-

ing load. With this money, Stanford is able "to provide researchers with good graduate students as assistants. This relieves the
professor of glass-blowing chores and permits him to work more
efficiently."

Continues Terman: "You end up with trained students and
better teachers. Young people grow intellectually very rapidly
when sufficient research grants and allocations are available."

The Stanford official noted that it is now possible to get as
much as $100,000 for an important research project. "This has
completely reoriented the attitude of academic researchers, and
faculty members are now able to pick out the scientifically most
important projects, rather than being hamstrung by costs."

At the University of Chicago, where this year's government
funding of research projects will total close to $26 million, re-
actions are similar. Graduate-level education has been enhanced
"immeasurably," says a spokesman, and he calls participation in
research by a student "an educational process." If the government closed its R&D funding doors, "we would have to close
ours," he says.

At Columbia, where Federal support of research projects has
grown at a rate of $4 million annually since World War II,
officials credit much of the rise in national academic standards
to Washington's support of research and development.

"It makes possible research apparatus which would be much
too costly for any one school to purchase," says a Columbia
spokesman. "And more important, it attracts and keeps top professors, graduate students, and researchers in the universities."
Cut down government funds and "you'd see a flight of talent
from colleges that would destroy higher education in the United
States for a long time to come," he adds.

At the University of Illinois, Ross Martin, director of the Engineering Experiment Station, admits to some problems in control-
ling government-sponsored research. "We have just faded out on
some cases where the government agency wanted to run the
project by long-distance."

Mainly, though, Illinois' experience with government R&D
grants has been excellent, says Martin. "It's enabled the univer-

sity to engage in a much broader research program, it's raised the caliber of professors and graduate students, and in the process it's produced a wealth of new important scientific data," he observes.

At both California Institute of Technology and Massachusetts Institute of Technology, two top sources of engineering brains, authorities also point to scope, quality, and level of basic research in the United States and credit it in large part to Federal outlays.

"The increased funds available for research in the colleges," says Cal Tech President L. A. DuBridge, "have enabled the colleges to expand their scientific research and teaching to a level of excellence far beyond what could have been obtained without external support."

General James McCormack, vice president of MIT, agrees. "Graduate study would be getting almost nowhere without funding from the government," he maintains.

II. The Squeeze

Officials at colleges and universities not on the government's top research contractor list have few arguments with such claims. What they do find, however, is that not only is it harder to compete with the giants in searching out new grants, but that the sheer volume of paperwork in dealing with the government is a burden almost too heavy to bear.

At MIT, Harvard, and most other schools receiving the bulk of research funds, offices have been set up to handle paperwork between the professors and the government. This gives the school power at the front office to reject research projects that don't give schools the academic freedom that they may demand.

Smaller colleges, with less centralization of government research contracts, often have failed to exert such control—with unfortunate results. In recent months, though, a number have moved to correct this failing. Two recent examples were Georgia Institute of Technology, which annually gets $5.5 million in Federal research funds, and Boston University, with $6.2 million.

"We've discovered we need a marriage broker between the faculty and the government," is how a B.U. official puts it. Both

B.U. and the Georgia Board of Regents will appoint a director of research to act as middleman. The appointment may not completely clear the situation, but it may eliminate some friction that builds up when too many staff researchers apply for competing government grants.

One widespread complaint is the problem of indirect, overhead research costs—something that even the wealthiest universities find difficult to bear.

The University of Pennsylvania's director of project research and grants, F. Haydn Morgan, bluntly states, "It actually costs Penn money every time it undertakes a new government research project because charges are inadequate for overhead. We never break even."

The same complaint is heard down the street in Philadelphia at the Drexel Institute of Technology. "The question is how much government research can we afford," says a spokesman.

The government puts a 25 per cent limit on overhead costs on research projects it sponsors. At Georgia Tech, the 25 per cent cut-off pays for only 45 per cent to 50 per cent of the overhead; the balance must come from state funds.

At the University of Southern California, which had $10 million in government research funds last year [1962], authorities tend to fault the government for disproportionate emphasis on the natural sciences. But government contracts are equal to 30 per cent of the school's total operating budget and have permitted considerable modernization and expansion. Major gripes centered about government auditing of research work and the disproportionate amount of lab space that government projects required.

USC admits graduate students are lured to the university with big government research contracts. "They stay on longer, putting in their extra time in the lab instead of out in the local gas station picking up needed extra money," says a Southern California spokesman.

But, with government work, professors inevitably find it more difficult to attend to graduate teaching, and assistants are forced to carry more and more of the actual instruction load.

III. Blank Areas

Cleveland educators score government research on another front. The over-all influence has been growth- and mission-oriented, they charge. Basic research is neglected; the humanities are neglected. "Most important to government spenders is to get a man on the moon, find a way to cure juvenile delinquency, or pinpoint a cure for cancer," complains one official.

At Western Reserve University, where $9.7 million of the $10.8 million slated for research will come from Washington, William R. Heston, vice president for research, blames government demands for "specific objectives" for the shortage of true scientific research in the United States today. Says one of his associates: "How can you cost-account education?"

At Case Institute of Technology, a spokesman voices the same complaint. "Congress," he says, "isn't interested in education *per se.* Everything is aimed at its own specific goal."

IV. Big-Brother Threat

Baldwin-Wallace College President Alfred B. Bonds, Jr., sees the government's tremendous outlays in university research as a serious threat to small independent private colleges. "Already there has been a sharp departure from the basis of private education with its high degree of academic freedom," he says.

Dr. Harry H. Ransom, chancellor of the University of Texas, agrees. The most important, yet subtle, shift in values and emphasis that has resulted is a lessening of institutional "flexibility," he says. In an attempt to prevent any such change at Texas, Ransom has set up a ten-year R&D plan with no use of Federal money.

For the same reason, Rice University at Houston has established its research sponsor program, supported by corporate grants. This gives President Kenneth S. Pitzer from $150,000 to $200,000 yearly to use as he sees fit.

Dr. Pitzer's explanation for the back-up fund raises an important point. "This matter of getting approval for a proposal raises problems, since you can't help being influenced by what you think the funding agency will think. . . . Long-shot experiments are the ones awfully hard to get approval for, and it's harder for younger, unknown professors to get grants than for well-established names to win them."

Another harmful effect of government research money, critics charge, is the competition it is causing for available Federal funds.

V. The Scramble

Such a race raises the question of "quality gap" among institutions. Since a hard core of twenty colleges and universities virtually monopolizes Federal R&D money—and these were the institutions with faculties of highest repute before the research boom began—the question has been raised whether the government in a backhand way is, in effect, subsidizing increasing mediocrity of already mediocre institutions.

And some educators are wondering if the mediocre school isn't faced with an increasingly difficult job in attracting—or even keeping—top-quality people.

Not only has it caused a race for research money, but the increase in government R&D funds has also set off a talent scramble within individual institutions. Top talent is always hard to find, and the various disciplines are competing with each other for good graduate students.

Says Dr. Charles F. Squires, associate dean of arts and sciences at Texas A&M: "My medical friends tell me they are distressed by the quality of the talent they're getting; it's simply being attracted to other fields."

SOME LESSONS FROM THE BERKELEY CRISIS [5]

It isn't often that a great university suddenly goes smash, yet that is what happened to the Berkeley campus during the first week of last December [1964]. During that week the University of California (Berkeley), numbering 27,000 students, 12,000

[5] From "A Special Supplement: Berkeley and the Fate of the Multiversity," by Sheldon S. Wolin and John H. Schaar, who teach political science at the Berkeley campus of the University of California. New York Review of Books. p 15-18. Mr. 11, '65. Reprinted from The New York Review of Books. Copyright © 1965, The New York Review.

faculty and nonacademic employees, numerous research laboratories, institutes, old-fashioned classrooms, and boasting an annual budget of $60 million, suffered an almost total collapse. Campus authority vanished, academic routines were reduced to a shambles, and the prophecy of Mario Savio [leader of the student movement] was fulfilled: the "machine" came to a "grinding halt."

This brought to a climax a succession of events, each more astonishing than the one before, which had kept the University in a continuous ferment since mid-September. It is no surprise that those outside the University community have been unable to make sense of these events, for even the participants themselves often had trouble in understanding their own behavior. Many of the student demands and tactics seemed outlandish and more appropriate to Birmingham than to Berkeley. The responses of University officials wavered between treating the student movement as a Children's Crusade, a Communist conspiracy, and "a civil rights panty raid" (as one administrator saw it). The most outlandish behavior, however, came neither from the students nor the myopic deans, but from those specifically charged with governing the institution. Supporting the seemingly invulnerable institution in its moment of crisis was a broad array of interested and powerful elements: the Governor and Board of Regents; interest groups which had long prospered from the services and needs of the University; and a suspicious and hostile public, misled by the local press into believing that agitators were destroying the University and moved by an urge to punish the young for their seeming lack of gratitude for all the advantages which a generous citizenry had given them. Yet, the authority of the University crumpled under the pressure of a few thousand students who had no other power than the moral courage to say No before the colossus and the tactical skill to say it at the right time and in unison.

Absurd it may have been, but it was not trivial. The events destroyed some illusions about contemporary education and disclosed the depths of the antagonism between a generation which has all but contracted out of the affluent society, and the perfect dehumanized expression of that society, the large-scale organization, which transmutes knowledge, energy, and money into technological miracles—the perfect artifact for multiplying change so as to drown out purpose. In a society which values growth and material power above all else, and which cannot comprehend why rebellion and discontent should flourish amidst plenty and opportunity, it was astonishing to observe the students making a moral protest in defense of traditional rights which their elders could not take seriously and in defense of the principles of a liberal education which their elders had mislaid somewhere among the many other functions of the "multiversity." The crisis demonstrated that socially useful functions, no matter how competently performed, are no substitute for moral authority.

Origins of Free Speech Movement

Had the students not succeeded in creating an instrument to convert their moral outrage into power, their protests would have died unheard. The Free Speech Movement came into existence during the first week in October, and from then on it enjoyed a near monopoly on the expression of protest. It attracted widespread support and enlisted the energies of thousands of students for the numerous tasks demanded by a political struggle. Although its wide support gave it a heterogeneous quality—stretching from the radical right to the radical left—its political style was uniquely expressive of the new generation. It was highly conscious of political and social issues; its language was radical and its tactics aggressive, but pervaded by a novel blend of moralism and impudence ("liberal" and "fink" were almost synonymous, "textbook" was made to sound like "pornography"). There is no doubt that there were devious motives among its leaders; that occasionally they became intoxicated by their sudden power and made noises as if they intended to smash the whole system; that here and there extreme leftists were to be found. Yet it would be a serious mistake to suggest, as other writers have, that the entire crisis was fabricated and dominated by subversives or riff-raff. It has been well established that most of the followers were intelligent students who were novices in political action.

The sacrifices of many who were willing to place their careers on the line, the spontaneity of their indignation, the warm fellowship of their movement, and their unfailing good humor were too real to be explained by subterranean conspiracies. Those who believe that, by definition, a problem does not exist if it can be shown that radicals are somehow involved, are not about to acknowledge the dominating idealism of the movement. At bottom the unbelievers must fear that the situation is really worse than even the conspiracy theory suggests: if it is possible for so many—faculty and students alike—to be duped by so few, then the condition of one of the world's greatest universities is more hopeless than even its critics charge.

The many issues raised during these chaotic months can be classified under two broad headings. First, there were political and constitutional issues centering around whether the University should place any but the most minimal restrictions upon the exercise of political rights by students on campus, and whether the University should restrain and discipline political acts or advocacy performed on the campus but leading to illegal acts off the campus (e.g., a political rally called on campus to organize an illegal sit-in at a hotel). Historically, the administration had based its highly restrictive policies on a provision of the state constitution requiring that "The University shall be entirely independent of all political or sectarian influence and kept free therefrom in the appointment of its Regents and in the administration of its affairs." This became the justification for prohibiting political advocacy and activity on campus, for defining what activities were political, and for denying the use of campus facilities for organizing off-campus political actions. The policy of the administration was determined primarily by the desire to prevent the involvement of the University in public controversy.

The students' general contention was that they should have the same political rights on campus that they enjoyed as citizens off the campus, and that determinations of the legality of off-campus actions should be reserved exclusively to the courts. In addition, the students argued that the constitutional provision upon which the administration relied was intended to prevent the

University itself from becoming involved in politics, and to prevent the governors of the University from applying political criteria in the conduct of University affairs, but was not intended to deny students the right to engage in political action not involving the name of the University. Finally, the students argued that the administration had been highly arbitrary in the day-to-day application of its rules.

Alienation of Students

An overwhelming majority of the faculty was gradually persuaded that the student argument was generally correct. As early as October 13, the faculty had affirmed its support for "maximum freedom for student political activity" and on December 8 formally resolved that there should be only minimal regulations on the *form* of political speech and action on campus, no University controls on the *content* of expression, and no University sanctions on the off-campus political activities of its students.

The second broad range of issues related to the University itself. The gross size and population of the campus, the numerous research and service functions carried on, its intimate connections with outside interests have transformed the old categories of "teacher" and "academic community" into "researcher" and "multiversity" or "knowledge factory" (the last phrases are those of its President). Unlike many private institutions, Berkeley's character was not established by a founder or given shape by a religious sect determined to bring piety and learning to a rude society. Ungraced by traditions, its graduates lack a distinctive stamp. Above all, identities are hard to come by and definitions difficult to pronounce when an institution is determined to gear its life and growth to the needs of an ever-expanding society, or at least to the needs of society's most powerful and clamorous parts. In *The Uses of the University* [see excerpt in "The Frantic Race to Remain Contemporary," Section I, above], President Clark Kerr writes that the multiversity has "no prophet to proclaim its vision; no guardian to protect its sanctity." The clear implication is that the multiversity dare not risk self-definition. It must remain "as confused as possible for the sake of the preservation of the whole uneasy balance" among the interests and pressures that make up its environment. If it is the multiversity's nature not to have a nature, there is comfort in knowing that it is "an imperative . . . rooted in the logic of history." The beauty of an imperative is that it provides a "justification" for virtually anything, including the mish-mash of activities that have found a home in the multiversity.

Kerr's realization that the condition of the multiversity's existence is also the source of its weakness imports an element of desperation into his analysis. His use of industrial metaphors disguises the inherent anarchy of the multiversity system. There is a touch of melancholy in his conclusion that "the task is to keep this lawlessness within reasonable bounds." In the end the university is reduced to being a puppet, twitching to stimuli it cannot control, powerless to set its own direction. "The process cannot be stopped. The results cannot be foreseen. It remains to adapt."

If one is startled by this confession of drift by the head of the enterprise, how much more unprepared one is for his cynicism. The university is characterized as "a mechanism held together by administrative rules and powered by money." The faculty is "a series of individual . . . entrepreneurs held together by a common grievance over parking." For all their sprightliness, these epigrams sag—melancholy testimony that the realist is second to none in his illusions. Their author is the same man who early in the crisis denied that a "freedom of speech issue" existed and who, after the faculty voted overwhelmingly to eliminate restrictions on the content of expression, demeaned the motives of that distinguished body by attributing its action to petty jealousy towards the other campuses in the system.

An examination of the pattern of events shows how great is the distance and how difficult the communication between those who make the multiversity's rules and those who must live by them.

The controversy opened on an appropriate note. On September 14, the administration blandly announced that a narrow strip of land at the entrance to the campus was really University property and not, as previously assumed, the property of the city (uncertain as to its own identity the multiversity has never been sure where it ends and the world begins). This strip had been the locus of student political activity. Since it was assumed to lie outside the campus, University regulations restricting political activity did not apply. Without consulting the students, the administration closed off the main outlet for political energies, claiming at first that these activities interfered with pedestrian traffic, but later reaffirming its position that "University facilities may not, of course, be used to support or advocate off-campus political or social action."

Vacillation by University Officials

The students immediately formed a united front, ranging from Goldwaterites to Socialists, to urge the restoration of a free-speech area and the modification of the rules. The Chancellor [Edward W. Strong] then issued a "clarification," the first of a long series that came to follow a familiar pattern of concession and contradiction, giving an over-all impression of weakness. The students were allowed to use the steps of the administration building, Sproul Hall, as a free-speech area and to man tables on "the strip," but not for political purposes. The students proceeded to ignore this last restriction, and the administration to ignore the violations. Tables were set up and political speeches given in forbidden areas. Again the Chancellor gave ground and permitted students to support candidates in the November elections and to take stands on state propositions. This gave something to everybody: the students might oppose an amendment repealing the state fair housing law, while the University could continue its efforts for an educational bond issue. Characteristically, the Chancellor followed these concessions with a show of firmness which he then undercut by his own actions. He stated on September 28 that the matter was "closed," but then had his deans select eight students, including three leaders, from among hundreds who claimed to have violated the regulations. The eight were suspended "indefinitely"—a penalty unknown to University rules.

This led to the first great blow-up: On October 1 a large rally formed in front of Sproul Hall. A police car taking to jail a person charged with manning a table unlawfully was surrounded and stranded in a sea of students. Mario Savio, considerately barefoot, mounted the car and harangued the crowd. Two hundred students then entered Sproul for a sit-in. Faculty efforts at mediation were blocked by the Chancellor's stubborn insistence that regulations and disciplinary measures were not negotiable. As the tension continued into the next day, a faculty group by-passed the Chancellor and persuaded President Kerr of the need for compromise. This began the gradual eclipse of the Chancellor by the President, thus underscoring the fact that each campus of the multiversity lacks autonomy and is headed only by an expendable functionary, suitably called "the chief campus officer." An agreement was reached with Kerr, but not before he had summoned five hundred police and threatened to have them disperse the crowd unless an agreement was reached. The students agreed to halt the demonstrations and in return the University agreed to restore the privileges of certain suspended groups, to submit the cases of the eight to a committee of the Academic Senate, to drop its charges against the man encapsulated in the police car, and to establish a committee of faculty, students, and administrators to study the rules.

The agreement was a disaster. Neither administration nor students acquitted themselves with honor. The Chancellor appointed ten of the twelve members of the tripartite committee without seeking recommendations from either students or faculty. He also assigned the cases of the eight to a committee of his own choosing, not to one appointed by the Academic Senate. In response to protests, Kerr again intervened to retrieve the situation. The cases of the eight were transferred to a committee established by the Senate. This committee, after hearings, recommended that six of the students be reinstated immediately. A six-week suspension was recommended for the other two. The committee's report was also highly critical of the administration's procedures.

The Chancellor announced that he would not respond to these recommendations until the following month.

Meanwhile, the tripartite committee foundered. The truculence of the FSM representatives, combined with the refusal of the administration's spokesmen to surrender disciplinary powers over "illegal" advocacy, created an impasse. The FSM resumed the manning of tables. The Chancellor then dissolved the tripartite committee on the grounds that the students had violated the agreement of October 2. From November 9 to November 20, the students continued to violate the regulations while the administration enforced them selectively, now citing seventy students for infractions, now ignoring massive violations.

On November 20 the Board of Regents, highest authority in the entire university system, met. The Board is wondrously representative of the genius of the multiversity. It would be difficult to design a more attractive target for students nurtured on the C. Wright Mills doctrine of the conservative power elite. It is composed mainly of high politicians, wealthy financiers, industrialists and businessmen, and the remarkable Max Rafferty [state superintendent of public instruction]. Kerr persuaded the Board to overturn its prohibition against all on-campus political activity and advocacy, although the ban against "illegal advocacy" was retained. The Board's *quid pro quo* was a recommendation that students who had violated the rules during the past three months should be disciplined. It also dealt with the cases of the eight students and recommended reinstatement of the whole group but refused to expunge the charges against them.

The Regents nearly restored peace. The FSM was badly split; a sit-in in Sproul on November 23 was called off after a few hours, indicating that the remaining area of controversy was too limited to be inflammatory. Just when most faculty and students were resuming normal routines, the Chancellor restored chaos by a master stroke of stupidity, bad timing, and injustice. He sent letters to four students, including three top leaders of FSM, informing them that the University intended to bring charges for actions committed eight weeks earlier. By reopening a matter which everyone had assumed to be closed, he, with one blow, revived FSM, outraged the faculty, and focused the question in its starkest terms: how is it possible to justify an authority so . . . insensitive to the spirit of an academic institution?

Two days later, on December 2, nearly eight hundred students filed into Sproul Hall for the climactic sit-in. The next day Governor Brown called in six hundred police to clear the students from the building and hustle them off to jail. The faculty rallied to the students: cars were provided to return them from jail and a bail fund was set up and quickly oversubscribed. While all this was going on, the graduate students had organized a strike which successfully halted most classes for two days. The students had fulfilled their vow: the machine was stopped.

The Faculty Reacts

Up to this point, the faculty as a body had remained relatively detached, though a few individuals had occasionally been involved in the controversy. But now the collapse of authority and the sight of nearly six hundred armed policemen shocked the faculty into the recognition that it alone was left to pick up the pieces. For a time, the faculty forgot its lust for research, its shameful neglect of teaching, its acquiescence in the bureaucratization of the University. Setting aside the ethos of power and growth, the faculty stirred to ancestral memories of the ideal of a community of scholars bound together in the spirit of friendly persuasion and pledged to truth rather than abundance. It had been clear all along that while the students' protests were directed against the administration, their entreaties were directed to the faculty, but it took a shattering experience to restore the faculty memories of fellowship with the students. Now that its collective conscience was awakened, the faculty found the energy and vision necessary for the task of reconstruction. . . .

One line of faculty action was in response to the impotence of the Chancellor whose withdrawal and increasing isolation left the campus leaderless. A committee of departmental chairmen was formed to impress upon the President the gravity of the situation. After exhausting negotiations, the chairmen wrung from the President and a group of Regents a promise not to add University punishment to court sentences of the sit-ins. It is symbolic that the chairmen's group and the Regents never talked face-to-face. University rules forbid faculty members from making direct approaches to the Regents; hence the two parties were closeted in separate rooms of an airport motel and the President plied between them.

The amnesty was a necessary precondition for resolving the crisis, but the Kerr-Chairmen Agreement was silent on the fundamental questions of political freedom which the students had been raising. That silence provoked outbursts of protest when the President and a distinguished faculty member presented the terms of the armistice to the campus community assembled in the Greek Theater. Moreover, their rhetoric of affluence and order revealed a fatal ignorance of the yearnings and commitments of the present generation of students. ("Today we decide whether we shall move ahead productively and in peace. . . . This community has been divided not so much on ends as on means. . . . We must seek added funds. . . . We must face external investigations. . . . We must face . . . a transition from the extensive growth of the past century to the intensive growth of the indefinite future—for growth must never stop.")

Resolving the Free Speech Issue

Throughout November several groups of faculty members had been formulating proposals to meet the problem of student political activities, but the events of December 2 generated the passion necessary to unite the faculty. On December 4 an impromptu faculty meeting was called and the discussion there disclosed a deep sentiment among the vast majority for policies that would set no limits upon the *content* of expression and only such minimal restraints upon the *forms* of expression as were necessary to the performance of ordinary University functions. The faculty was also becoming persuaded that the intricate legal questions surrounding "illegal" speech and "conspiracy" were not the proper business of any university authority.

On December 8 these sentiments, now refined in the form of resolutions, were brought before the Academic Senate and passed by a vote of 824-115. The resolutions provided that: (1) only the "time, place, and manner" of on-campus political activity should be regulated to "prevent interference with the normal functions of the University"; (2) the content of speech was not to be restricted; (3) off-campus political activities should not be subject to University regulations; (4) disciplinary questions arising out of the minimal regulations in (1) should be handled by a faculty committee, i.e., the administration was not to touch such matters.

Two additional resolutions were passed. One created an Emergency Executive Committee to act for the faculty in further matters arising out of the crisis, and the other called for a committee to study the question of how the faculty might make itself more effective in the general governance of the University. The importance of these changes was quickly demonstrated, for the next encounter took place elsewhere, at the December 18 meeting of the Board of Regents.

The Regents have final power in almost every area of University affairs. Usually their meetings deal with ordinary matters of University business, but this was to be no ordinary meeting. More like a summit conference, it was surrounded by an atmosphere of urgency and intense public concern. What occurred is not easy to reconstruct, because part of the meeting was secret; what was decided is not entirely clear because of the muddled language of the public statement issued later. It seems that the Regents have finally recognized the First and Fourteenth Amendments, and that henceforth students will be allowed maximum political freedom on the campus. It is clear that students may now use campus facilities for organizing off-campus actions. However, the Regents continued to balk at the use of campus facilities for mounting illegal off-campus actions, and hence reserved authority to discipline students in such matters. The Regents also refused to devolve upon the faculty final authority over student disciplinary cases in political questions.

Despite the face-saving vagueness of their formulations, the Regents had come far since September. Their allusion to the First and Fourteenth Amendments was a tacit confession that most University rules affecting speech and action were unconstitutional, and their decision not to punish the arrested students raised the hope that eventually they would relinquish jurisdiction over cases where off-campus actions turn out to be illegal. Moreover, in announcing their willingness to consult with students and faculty to improve campus rules, the Regents recognized what the faculty had sensed earlier: students must be viewed as participating members of the academic community. . . .

As matters now stand, the faculty and students have gained most of the objectives contained in the December 8 resolutions. Assuming that good sense prevails among the parties, that the few zealots in the legislature do not persist in their announced aim of firing masses of students and faculty, and that the impending trial of the sit-ins does not reopen old wounds, the prospects for honorable peace are good. But peace is not necessarily the same as normality, for the events of the first semester cut too deep to permit a restoration of the old ways. A university is in the process of being redefined. Its President has recently proclaimed that "The primary responsibility of the university is the education of its students. A second major responsibility is research . . ." (a draft of the University's ten-year program made last fall had no mention of "primary" emphasis upon education). But the basic element in all redefinitions is the new breed of students who have appeared on the Berkeley campus.

Published accounts of the student movement have radically distorted its character. Some of these accounts have been almost delusional in quality. There is, for example, Professor Lewis Feuer's denial that there were any genuine issues at stake and his claim that very few genuine students were involved in the controversy. He attributes the uprising to the powers of a handful of crackpots, political extremists, drug addicts, and sexual libertines —most of them, thank God, not students at all, but spoiled personalities, tormented members of that underground Berkeley community of *lumpen*-intellectuals—who managed to dupe thousands of innocent and true students into believing that there were real issues, thereby capturing the ever-present hostility of the young against their elders and mobilizing it into a "generational uprising." Less imaginative men than Feuer have characterized the movement as the subversive work of leftist plotters. In this view, the campus will not find peace until it surgically removes these diseased members from the student body politic.

A New Breed of Students

Another way to avoid the challenge of understanding is to concentrate all attention upon one aspect of the reality, and then to interpret that reality in very narrow categories. Specifically, this approach characterizes the behavior and tactics of the students as riotous and irresponsible, and condemns them as illegal, thereby foreclosing the issues. Some of the students' actions were illegal, but that still leaves open the questions of whether they were necessary and morally justified. Furthermore, and contrary to the impression spread by the mass media, the students were not tempestuous and violent. With few exceptions, they behaved with dignity and restraint.

All of these accounts dissolve the real problem into a vapor of fantasies congenial to the commentator. None of them recognizes that there were real students asserting real grievances within an institutional setting that had in fact become pathological. As President Kerr himself noted, the students have been "restless" for some time. An adequate account must take a serious look at the sources of that restlessness.

For some time now, the students, especially the undergraduates, have felt themselves to be an alien presence within the multi-versity, an "Other Academia" analogous to the "Other America," ill-fed, ill-housed and ill-clothed not in the material sense, but in the intellectual and spiritual senses. As the multiversity has climbed to higher and higher peaks of research productivity, material riches, and bureaucratic complexity, the students have fallen into deeper and deeper abysses of hostility and estrangement. The students' own favorite word for their condition is "alienation," by which they mean a number of things, and especially a sense of not being valued members of a genuine intellectual and moral community. Their feeling is grounded in reality.

The architects of the multiversity simply have not solved the problem of how to build an institution which not only produces knowledge and knowledgeable people with useful skills, but which also enriches and enlightens the lives of its students— informing them with the values of the intellect, preparing them to serve as the guardians of society's intellectual honesty and political health, arming them with the vision by which society seeks its own better future. It is the performance of these latter tasks that distinguishes a genuine educational community from a mere research factory and training institution. Hence, as Harold Taylor [former President of Sarah Lawrence College] has said, "The mark of a true university is whether or not it takes its students seriously."

By any reasonable standard, the multiversity had not taken its students seriously. At Berkeley, the educational environment of the undergraduate is bleak. He is confronted throughout his entire first two years with indifferent advising, endless bureaucratic routines, gigantic lecture courses, and a deadening succession of textbook assignments, and bluebook examinations testing his grasp of bits and pieces of knowledge. All too often the difference between the last two years of a student's education and the first two is chronological rather than qualitative. It is possible to take a B.A. at Berkeley and never talk with a professor. To many of the students, the whole system seems a perversion of an educational community into a factory designed for the mass processing of men into machines. The image is a bit excessive, to be sure, but like any good caricature this one distorts reality in order to clarify it. A great many faculty members have acknowledged the essential justice of the students' case against the multiversity, and have confessed their own not-so-small contribution to the malaise. Faculty conversation at Berkeley is now haunted by remorseful allusions to the bleak realities of student life.

The reality seems all the bleaker by contrast with the glowing expectations which students are now bringing to the university. Young people today are conditioned from the earliest age to see "education" as the magic key to all the delectable things. They come to college in search, not merely of knowledge, but of salvation. College is the real thing, they are told, and when the real thing turns out to look a lot like the sham they left behind, they are understandably distressed.

It costs relatively little money to attend the University of California, but unlike most other state universities, California has high admission standards. The freshmen class is selected from the top 10 per cent of high school seniors. This means that not only are the students of high average intelligence, but that they also have worked hard and kept "clean" throughout their high school years. Furthermore, Cal students, like all others, bring with them to college youth's natural exuberance, but relatively little of this energy is drained off through the customary and "safe" channels of sports, organized social life, and seasonal bacchanals. Most of the energy finds other outlets.

Characteristics of the Berkeley Student

Most of the students live in private accommodations, and their private lives do seem quite experimental and free—though not as orgiastic as the fevered imaginations of some professors and deans would suggest. More importantly, over the past decade the students have become increasingly serious—about themselves, their studies, and their society. But there is still a lot of energy left, and at Berkeley, unlike most other American colleges, a good bit of this is poured into political and social causes. For example, Berkeley in particular, and the San Francisco Bay Area in general, have sent more young people to the South in the struggle for racial justice than any other place except New York. The word has gone out: things are happening at Berkeley. This reputation acts as a magnet, drawing young people with activist yearnings from all over the nation to Berkeley. The events of last semester, with all the publicity they gained, will increase this magnetic attraction—a thought horrifying enough to bring a dean to consider resigning his post.

Beyond the immediate attractions of a lively campus, many students today, especially those in the humanities and social sciences, are aware of the shortcomings of their society and are passionately looking for authentic values to replace what they perceive as the phony slogans and spiritual tawdriness of so much of the public rhetoric and action of our time. Few of them come to college with an ideology, nor do they seek one while there. Rather, theirs is an ethic of sincerity and personal encounter. They take ideals seriously, and are quick to detect evasion, posturing, and double-think. If their conception of the educational process is somewhat romantic and wooly—tending to equate the exchange of impressions and sentiments with learning, impatient with discipline, and inclined to rush off after a dozen exciting novelties at once—it is still more attractive than the emphasis on utility and training favored in the multiversity establishment. The latter is a bleakness of spirit, closed and immobile; while the former is a plentitude of spirit, open and vital. Such students constitute a university's most valuable resource, and it is a delight and a privilege to teach them. There were a great many such students, graduate as well as undergraduate, involved in the happenings at Berkeley. Given all the loose talk about student "riots" and "radicals," it is necessary to emphasize this point.

There were radicals among the leadership of the FSM, but there is no evidence to indicate that the movement's leaders were the slaves of ideologies that blinded them to reality, or led them into attempts to subvert the true purposes of their mass following —which, to say it again, were freedom of political expression and educational reform. Furthermore, the vast majority of the students shared the goals of the FSM, and a near majority also supported their direct-action tactics. The "radicalism" of this mass following consisted in little more than devotion to some traditional principles which their elders had taught them, plus that impatience with the conservatism of the old which the young ought to have. Radical ideology, then, mattered little in the events at Berkeley. What mattered far more was a clear-eyed and courageous response to concrete, felt injustices.

There were no riots. Save for the incident of the "captured" police car, the mass rallies, sit-ins, and the student strike were all conducted with admirable dignity and calm. There were a few scattered episodes of excessive behavior by individuals under extreme stress. There were many intemperate words. Many University rules and a few state laws were broken.

All of this is regrettable, but understandable, and not unjustifiable. These students were acting in a situation where, time and again, officials refused to listen to them, behaved whimsically and punitively, and altogether gave the impression that the student cause was without justice. The students responded with the only methods that could make the administration listen, and many of them showed a clearer appreciation than their elders of the moral burdens involved in the use of pressure tactics within an academic setting. What happened at Berkeley cannot be understood as the delinquent outbursts of fanatics and ungrateful rebels. These students broke the rules and the law in an agonizing effort to compel an administration which, by its unwillingness to listen to their just claims and to treat them as participating members of a community of the intellect, inevitably brought about its own moral downfall and forfeited its claim to willing obedience. To many of the students, such conduct left no alternative but direct action.

The events of the past semester have not cast a foreboding shadow over the future of education at Berkeley. It is clear to many of us here that the students reminded us of some basic values that were disappearing in the thoughtless rush for the future. Very much of what they did had to be done before anyone would listen. The result is, at this moment, a climate of respect and concern that offers more promise than has been present in a long time that the future of this University can be a noble one.

III. TODAY'S STUDENTS: A NEW BREED?

EDITOR'S INTRODUCTION

Why are so many young Americans bent upon attending the "college of their choice" today? To play varsity football? To join a fraternity or sorority? To partake of the "collegiate way of life" at the expense of their parents?

Though such factors undoubtedly continue to motivate some students, indications are that genuinely intellectual considerations are coming increasingly to the fore. We are, observers say, in the midst of the "serious sixties" on campus. Students are going to college to learn. As never before in history, perhaps, they are seriously engaging in intellectual pursuits. Today's Big Man on Campus is the college intellectual who takes his politics as seriously as his studies. His sexual code may be more relaxed than in the past, but his sense of concern for the "rightness" of what is going on in the world around him seems stronger.

All this is not to say, of course, that a love of knowledge for its own sake has become the primary motivation of the nation's youth. Idealism abounds, but it is tempered by a basic appreciation of reality. In our increasingly complex, industrialized society, more and more jobs are being restricted to those with college degrees. Never before have so many young Americans attended college, but it is also true that never before has a college education meant as much in terms of opportunity and material reward as it does today. Consequently, pressures are great—pressures to be admitted in the first place and, once having been admitted, to emerge successfully and, if possible, at the head of the class. Such pressures no doubt contribute to an atmosphere of seriousness.

The three articles in this section give a profile of today's student, his attitudes, behavior, and ambitions. In the first, the editors of *Newsweek,* together with pollster Louis Harris, range far and wide across the campuses of the nation recording how

students feel about themselves and their environment. Readers
may be surprised to learn that the present college generation is
less rebellious than headlines indicate. The second article, from
U. S. News & World Report, points up some of the ways in
which the current crop of undergraduates differs from its predecessors. And in the final article two free-lance writers examine
some of the pressures—mental and emotional—to which modern
students are subjected and the manner in which they react.

THE MOOD ON CAMPUS [1]

America's future has always belonged to its youth, but never
before have the young staked out so large a claim to America's
present. Not only are the young more numerous, they are more
influential. Healthier and wealthier, if not wiser, than their
predecessors, today's youthful tastemakers have stamped a vigorous imprint on popular entertainment, popular fashion, and the
popular idiom.

The young successfully "Beatle-ized" the nation, and many
think they may be about to "Berkeley-ize" it as well. After the
student sit-ins at the University of California, educators began
using the phrase "since Berkeley" in the same portentous tone
that physicists say "since Alamogordo."

Across the nation last week, from Ivy Yale to red-brick Brooklyn College to land-grant Kansas to Roman Catholic St. John's
University in New York, students once more were challenging
authority, and the authorities didn't know quite what to make of
it. At Berkeley itself, the cradle of the new restlessness, the
student rebellion almost claimed its most prominent and perhaps
unnecessary victim, Clark Kerr, president of America's greatest
public university.

Just as they thrust their way onto the center of the educational
stage, so too did students . . . thrust their way onto the center of
the political stage, sitting in at the White House in Washington
and marching on the courthouse in Selma. Clearly, this genera-

[1] From "Campus '65." *Newsweek.* 65:43-8+. Mr. 22, '65. Copyright, Newsweek,
Inc. March, 1965. Reprinted by permission.

tion demands to be heard as well as seen. But just what is it saying?

So far, the message is coming in loud, but not clear. One reason is that the college generation speaks in so many voices. In 1940 there were 1.5 million students in college. Today's enrollment: more than 5.2 million.

Once, when the college population was less numerous and less diverse, it could be characterized by catch phrases and slogans. In Paris in the twenties, Gertrude Stein could cast a baleful eye on the fated youth of her time and with melancholy certitude proclaim: "That's what you all are . . . a lost generation." And in the America of the fifties, novelist Clellon Holmes could sum up the aloofness and studied silence of some of his contemporaries by inventing the "beat" generation. But who today can sum up in a handful of words the manner and mood of this generation?

The contemporary coinage has a hollow ring—"explosive," "twisted," "cool," and "committed." That college students take a somewhat bemused view of the phrases and the phrasemakers is obvious from the headline in a recent edition of a mimeographed newspaper of satire published by students at Minnesota's Carleton College:

What's Bugging Them?
    ADULTS: THE TROUBLED GENERATION

Generalizations obviously will not suffice. Still, the adult world remains insatiably curious about what's bugging college students. It is almost as if parents and professors hope to glimpse a bit of America's future in the manner and mood of its youth.

To find out what is on the mind and in the heart of the college generation, *Newsweek* last month sent a team of interviewers from the staff of Louis Harris and Associates to a score of colleges across the country. . . .

From its hundreds of interviews and from the Harris poll, *Newsweek* has distilled the first comprehensive survey of Campus '65. Here, in the . . . pages that follow, the college generation looks at itself, its politics, its morals, its culture, and the world that it will inherit.

The Problem: Making the Grade

This college generation, like every one before it, glories in its own singularity, and well it may. It has galloped onto campus like a herd of unicorns from an old fable come true, the one about peace and prosperity. No youth, not in ancient Greece, enlightened Europe, nor modern America, has ever grown up under so strong a sun. There was the menace of the bomb, of course, but awfully abstract as bogeymen go. The economy had a fleeting dizzy spell, but today's students were babies and didn't notice. Men fought and died in bizarre Asian wars, but no one in the United States even bothered writing songs about them. Colonialism collapsed, a Communist empire arose, but the clamor never carried to their childhood bedrooms. Never have so many children been such complete strangers to famine, plague, want, or war. Theirs are the blessings of prosperity, theirs the spoils of peace.

They wear affluence as the children on Chinese houseboats wear life preservers, as part of their daily apparel. Their parents' annual median income is about $12,000. Sixty per cent of their fathers and half of their mothers are college educated. The students are well aware of their privileged status. Of those surveyed by *Newsweek*, 45 per cent thought it was easier being young today than in their parents' time, while 35 per cent thought it was harder.

They are not rebels, at least in the conventional sense. How many sports-car drivers, asks a North Carolina journalism student, have a social conscience? Not that they all drive sports cars. Bicycles crowd the campuses. Some of the hardier freshmen even walk. But whatever the degree of individual prosperity, their blessings are decidedly mixed.

"We haven't really been tested by war or depression," says Greg Lipscomb of Houston, president of the student body (24,000 strong) at the University of Texas. "We live very much in the present because we don't have to be overly concerned about the future." Today's collegians are confident about the future, less so about themselves. "Our generation was born into security and wealth," says Mary Grenier of Seattle, a senior at Seattle University. "We don't really understand hard work, many of us."

And college is hard work. Of those students polled who believed they have problems their parents never knew, 23 per cent cited the relentlessly increasing pressure for grades. What are the major pressures on students? Almost half gave the same answer: "Frustration over not being a superior student."

"Adults don't realize our mental strain," said Harry Hatton of Owego, New York, a freshman at New York's State University College at Cortland. "It is like a small revolution." There may be richer prizes than ever to be won, but competition for them is unprecedentedly fierce. Time's awasting as never before, and an exceedingly self-conscious generation ("I'm more aware of having a self-image," says an Indiana student) must constantly review its use of precious hours. . . .

In addition to dispensing knowledge, the campus has traditionally provided students with a breathing spell between the realization of their power and their testing of it in the world. Now the testing comes on campus, with grades. The college student's serene confidence in a prosperous future is predicated on the assumption that he will enter that future with a diploma, the *passe partout* of the modern world. So he must stay in college and meet its demands. "The pressure bit is pretty cumulative," says Francis J. Dever Jr., a Boston College freshman. "It seeps into about everything." The student is graded by his teachers, his parents, and himself. That can be a ruthless triumvirate, especially for the generation that grew up under Dr. Spock's permissive influence, the profoundly understood generation whose enlightened parents used Freud as a household word, much as their own parents used Flit.

Were the parents of today's collegians more permissive than the colleges are themselves? In an evaluation of parental attitudes, 80 per cent of the students thought they were "about right," 11 per cent thought their parents had been too strict, 8 per cent felt they had been too permissive. One per cent weren't sure. The youngsters of today may have unsuspected battles to fight, but not with the older generation.

Indeed, indications are that American youth is asking for a truce in the endless war between generations. Some difference may still persist: when students were asked how their parents had let them down, 27 per cent complained that they "won't recognize I've grown up." But this is not the stuff that wars are made of. And if spleen is in short supply, contrition's cup runneth over. How did the students feel they had let their parents down? Twenty-eight per cent berated themselves for doing poorly in their studies, 25 per cent for "not working to potential," and 20 per cent for not taking the direction their parents had wanted them to take.

So far, then, and tentatively, the emerging picture seems to indicate reassuring continuity, what with prosperous parents and purposeful, albeit overworked, progeny. The impression is enhanced by another statistic from the survey: 85 per cent of students interviewed declared themselves satisfied with college, only 12 per cent dissatisfied. This can hardly come as comfort to the Berkeley activists. It is as if today's American students were a reincarnation of the nineteenth-century Oxonian aristocrats, securely ensconced in their "sweet city with her dreaming spires."

But soft! The picture is patently cockeyed, or the wall on which it hangs is grievously out of plumb. For there is abundant evidence of a new discontinuity in the American culture, a veritable chasm between the undergraduates and the remainder of the civilized world. . . .

That generalized student satisfaction with college life, for example, contains within it some serious dissatisfactions. Though increasing population and growing organization of knowledge compel a trend toward ever bigger and multier multiversities, 60 per cent of the students preferred smaller schools. Thirty per cent opted for multiversities. Of those who favored small colleges, a leading 22 per cent cited the chance of more individual help, 18 per cent "informal contact," 16 per cent said small schools make it easier to "remain an individual, not a number." Only 8 per cent said it was easier to learn in a small college. By contrast, those who favored the multiversity cited mainly substantive reasons. They said multiversities are better equipped and provide a better-quality education.

Despite an intuitive belief that the small college is better for their souls, students suspect it represents a quickly fading reality. "The world," declares a senior at small, select Reed College, "is not a large Reed College." At Southwest Missouri State, James K. Jones of Springfield, Missouri, a senior in business management, says: "The impersonal attitude of the large university prepares you for the way the world is." Patricia Williams of Warren, Ohio, a senior at Hiram College, . . . [says that in a multiversity] "you're probably a number, but you're getting an education, and when you reach college age you shouldn't have to be babied."

This leads to another nagging question, that of the college acting *in loco parentis*, in the place of the parent. Many formal college traditions are tumbling: secret societies, fraternities, sororities, attendance at athletic events, the black-tie proms that used to bring Glenn Miller, Woody Herman, or Stan Kenton to the campus gym. Nevertheless, many schools still maintain another tradition: telling the student how to dress, how to behave, and when to come in at night. This usually goes down hard with the youngsters, these quasi-adults who ask: "Why are we treated like children in college?" Higher education induces a metamorphosis in most of its students, and change . . . involves pain.

Pain of so many bewildering sorts. The plight of the Wellesley girl who has "nothing graspable to say 'here I am and I have what you need.' " The pain of "senior panic" at most women's colleges, when the rush begins to land a husband. The pain of a new college trend, the trimester system, in which, says a University of Michigan senior, "things are happening too fast." The pain of an identity crisis—"I can travel, I can do what I want, but I find I don't know what I want out of life," says a Brooklyn College senior. . . .

Many students still sail blithely through school, untouched by such concerns. And some schools can still provide the sort of tranquil refuge appropriate to the task at hand (defined by Gail Heitler, a Wellesley senior from Denver, as "having four years to shut yourself off and come to terms with yourself"). Sometimes the refuge is so tranquil it seduces would-be activists away from their soap boxes and onto the greenswards or, worse yet, the ski slopes. At Colorado, Paul Danish, a self-styled radical and former editor of the student *Daily,* surveyed the majestic Rocky Mountains that provide a backdrop for the Boulder campus, then sighed: "How can you get totally excited and mad at a place like this? This is as close as you're going to get to nirvana."

Elsewhere, nirvana is not so close at hand. As the nation's colleges are swept along in the tide of technocracy and industrialism, the undergraduate's most telling complaint is about increasing emphasis on graduate studies and advanced research projects. Even at Harvard, where this animus is attenuated because so many Harvardians themselves (about four out of five) are bound for graduate schools, the sentiment was recently expressed in a *Crimson* editorial. Richard Cotton, former head of the paper, wrote that "perhaps the faculty will consider the reforms necessary to restore Harvard as a leading *educational* institution, as well as a leading center of scholarship."

Education, not scholarship. A discontinuity exists not only between parents and children, but between the malleable youngsters and "all the hard young men," as a Chicago historian called them, who have persevered in their specialities and learned how to run the world. Today's undergraduates cannot cope with the achievements of today's advanced scholars—the cyberneticists, biophysicists, neuropsychiatrists, systems analysts, astrophysicists, and other cortical cossacks now sweeping across the steppes of the intellect, who seem to understand, if anyone does, what the revolution in knowledge is all about.

Not that an undergraduate's world view must necessarily be dim. On campus after campus teachers chant the same refrain: today's high-school students come into college with already awesome sophistication, then expand their knowledge swiftly. But four years are only forty-eight months, no matter how deftly they are sliced. There is no time to learn the lessons, regurgitate them neatly into examination books, indulge in extracurricular activities (which are declining anyway), and also take the measure of the outside world. Interviews on campus, for instance, disclosed virtually no awareness of the population explosion's potentially stunning implications for new generations, including this one, in quest of the good life. The youngsters are still immature, in mind if not in spirit.

How, then, does the present college generation cope with its dilemma? Partly through direct action, partly through construction of its own set of workable, satisfying ideals, and partly through another tactic which is not necessarily what it seems to be. The direct political action . . . is the sort to be expected from a generation of "flaming moderates," as New York *Post* editor James A. Wechsler calls them. Like competent diplomatists, they deal soberly in the art of the possible. But their ideals, sometimes audacious and often conventional, are widely based.

When interviewers asked the students what they thought their lives would be like fifteen years from now, the replies were almost all of a piece—as neatly and bloodlessly laid out as the plot of a second-rate thriller. Only the thrills were missing. . . . "I'll be secure, financially. Married, have children, at least three," said an Indiana senior. For a Yale freshman life "will be somewhat similar to my parents', upper middle class, married with children, worried about getting into a rut." A Tennessee A&I coed saw herself as the "mother of five boys. Live in Pennsylvania. Live in a modern circular house that is completely automatic . . . will worry about nothing. Life is what you make it." . . .

Ill-disposed to shake the earth, confident in existing institutions such as banks, big corporations, the medical profession, and the scientific community, the college generation still had a surprise or two in store for its elders, especially in the matter of civil rights. Almost unanimously (98 per cent) they say they approve of Negro and white students eating in the same cafeteria. Ninety-three per cent approve of their living in the same dormitory, 85 per cent of their belonging to the same social club, 47 per cent of their dating a member of the other race, and 36 per cent approve of intermarriage. This contrasts with *Newsweek's* survey of white attitudes (October 21, 1963) which found no more than 10 per cent approving mixed dating or mixed marriages. For Mike Enwall, twenty-two, a Colorado University senior, a vision of a better society is "a place without 'niggers.' That really sums it up—a place where there are no phony differences between men."

Thus do the changes come, even in generations that find "the world they never made" rather well made at that. But this generation is in no rush to get out into the world, and here is where its aggregate behavior is most striking. A 52 per cent majority of graduating seniors interviewed said they intend to go on to graduate school. "Life has opened up new opportunities for us here, for meeting people and doing things," says Joe Rocchio, a student at the University of Rhode Island. "When graduation comes, I don't want to stop this. I don't want to work, come home and watch TV. I fear being put on a shelf, or being put on a path, like the rat maze, to go forward to the next piece of cheese."

Not only is the majority headed for graduate school, but a large plurality—36 per cent—of those interviewed said their first job would be in teaching or education, followed by 21 per cent in science and engineering. Never before has any American generation had the wherewithal to stay on the campus so long, and in such numbers. It is equally significant that this generation has decided to make use of its opportunity. . . .

The Activists—Protesting Too Much?

Casting a haughty eye on the American campus, Harvard's aristocratic Hasty Pudding club has chosen an appropriate theme for its annual satire this year. Its lavish musical . . . will portray the plight of the Protest Club at Poly Unsaturated U. The club's dilemma: having protested every conceivable ill, there is nothing left to protest.

In its heavy-handed way, "The Pud" is offering a timely commentary on the student-protest fever which seems to have reached epidemic national proportions. Since the first outbreak in Berkeley last fall, Michigan students have marched on President Harlan Hatcher's house demanding higher wages, and have picketed a movie-price increase, Columbia students have sat-in to support a union for the school-cafeteria employees, and at Fair Harvard itself, two hundred students recently paraded to express disapproval of United States policy in Vietnam.

No cause, it seems is without its student defenders these days. Just last week, Yalemen picketed the "publish or perish" law which cost a popular philosophy teacher a tenured appointment [see "The Tenure Problem," Section IV, below], and at Brooklyn College students protested that a "perform or perish" rule was behind the dismissal of a well-liked music professor. Nearby, at Roman Catholic St. John's University, students rallied for greater political freedoms on campus, protested priestly "paternalism," and even booed the name of their president, the Very Rev. Edward J. Burke. And the agenda of protest and picket shows no sign of ending. . . .

While the student protest signs may make easy satirical targets, more serious observers applaud the new spirit of campus militancy. At normally placid Kansas University, Chancellor W. Clarke Wescoe, himself a target of the protesters, declared he was "encouraged by the awakening of students we have seen in recent years." His comment came after 114 students were jailed for a sit-in at his office last week. They were protesting Wescoe's refusal to order immediate desegregation moves, including an end to racial discrimination by fraternities and sororities. After two days of demonstrations, Wescoe promised to negotiate the list of demands.

Yet for all the outbreaks of "campus political action," only a minority of students have been bitten hard by the Berkeley bug. And even when they resort to extralegal measures, what they seek are more direct channels to help resolve disputes. The *Newsweek* survey showed that only 18 per cent of those polled had actually picketed, though 56 per cent said they would for the right cause, indicating a substantial "protest potential."

The survey also showed the students were slightly more liberal than their parents—71 per cent voting for Mr. Johnson (his actual election percentage: 61)—but showed a predilection toward political nonalignment. Some 35 per cent called themselves independents, 33 per cent Democrats, and 24 per cent Republicans. Nearly half thought college had made them less dogmatic in their politics; significantly, students reported they had little confidence in either of the two major parties. On the major issue of the day—the United States commitment in Vietnam—their views were remarkably similar to those of their parents, with only 24 per cent advocating negotiation and withdrawal.

The majority of students who reject the activist scene may do so out of moderation—or just plain apathy. Some, self-centered perhaps, are too busy. Says Michigan *Daily* editor H. Neil Berkson: "Students just don't want to take part in outside activities, they worry more about getting into law or medical schools." . . .

For those who wish to nibble, campus politics is a lively smorgasbord which provides spice where there too often has been blandness. Among the national organizations, the current roster of clubs includes: the small W.E.B. DuBois clubs (Marxist), Progressive Labor Clubs (tend toward Maoism), Youth Socialist Alliance (Trotskyite), Young Peoples Socialist League (right-wing socialists), and the May Second Movement (antiwar in Vietnam). Students for a Democratic Society, a liberal-radical-socialist coalition, is the major power on the organized left, with 2,000 members on 60 campuses. The center is held by the Young Democrats, claiming 450,000 and the Young Republicans, reporting 135,000. The right is manned by Young Americans for Freedom (15,000), a small legion of nonpolitical Ayn Rand societies, and numerous unaffiliated Conservative and Individualist clubs. SNCC, the Student Nonviolent Coordinating Committee, is a major campus civil-rights organization across the country.

The right, while hardly the surging wave conservatives have dreamed of, has its footholds. Last fall, El Camino College, a sprawling car-campus in southern California of 13,500 students, voted narrowly for Goldwater. On the whole, the right tends to dress better, protest more politely, but no less vigorously. Commenting on the strength of the right at El Camino, a leading campus liberal noted: "It's hard to organize the liberals. They tend to want to sit around and discuss issues instead of getting out and doing something. That's one thing about the conservatives on campus—they're united by a common fear of spies and plots against them." At liberal Harvard, well-organized conservatives once infiltrated the Committee to Study Disarmament, and signaled their victory by changing the name to the Committee for Nuclear Weapons Development.

On the left, the passwords are "action" and "personal commitment." But commitment to what? Certainly not 1930's style political radicalism. "Protest is common, radicalism rare," notes one Midwestern liberal student. "These students don't read Marx," said one Berkeley Free . . . [Speech] Movement leader. "They read Camus." If they are rebels, they are rebels without an ideology, and without long-range revolutionary programs. They rally over issues, not philosophies, and seem unable to formulate or sustain a systemized political theory of society, either from the left or right. They express themselves through informal organizations mobilized for isolated ad hoc protests. A prime example, Berkeley's Free Speech Movement, eclipsed all the established groups when it campaigned for the right of students to engage in unrestricted political activity.

In the early 1960's, peace and nuclear testing held the primary attention of liberals on northern campuses. The apex was reached in February 1962, when Harvard's Tocsin Club and the national Student Peace Union, among others, brought 3,000 students to Washington for a peace march in the snow.

When the test ban was achieved in 1963, student attention turned toward civil rights, and, after the "rediscovery" of poverty, the needs of the poor in general. Perhaps students felt that, unlike the complex, distant world of foreign policy, these were problems which seemed susceptible to simple solutions, and, more importantly, offered opportunities for individual involvement. In this respect, the *Newsweek* survey shows that today's student is pessimistic about peace in his time. While a vast majority expected that their generation would land on the planets and cure cancer, three out of four despaired of eliminating the threat of war.

As part of the turn to domestic concerns, some students left the campus for Mississippi. Alex Capron, the former editor of Swarthmore's student paper, asks: "Isn't becoming engaged in the world outside part of becoming educated?" The answer of increasing numbers of students is Yes.

At affluent Harvard, 900 students this year have volunteered through the nonpolitical Phillips Brooks House to tutor underprivileged youngsters, teach in prisons, help out in hospitals and educational facilities. At North Carolina the student legislature recently inaugurated a program which will send 100 students into the field to teach remedial classes for Negroes. And the National Student Association estimates that some 70,000 students are involved in tutorial projects in urban and rural slums across the country.

While idealistic and humanitarian, some of these activities have served other needs as well. The Northern Student Movement found it had more trouble organizing tutoring for Negroes in big city slums than SNCC had recruiting volunteers for the South. The apparent reasons: the greater romance of facing danger in faraway Mississippi, and the simplicity of the issues there. Some of this romantic selflessness has also affected the enthusiastic response to the Peace Corps.

Given the pragmatic, personal bent of the activists, it was only to be expected they would eventually turn their eyes—and action—to the campus, the place they knew best and which affected them most. That was the meaning of Mario Savio and the FSM at Berkeley. The shock wave spread rapidly throughout the country. *Newsweek* found that 51 per cent of the students approved the FSM's tactics, and 38 per cent placed full blame for the trouble on the administration. Though sit-ins and pickets are one approved response, the revived interest in campus issues has also brought a resurgence in student government, an institution long in the doldrums. . . .

While students at the University of Florida at Gainesville rejected a Freedom Party which advocated integration and a "hometown poverty corps," Haverford recently elected Joe Eyer, who helped organize a group to send medical supplies to the Viet Cong, as its student body president. His program is typical. "We're somewhat antiquated here," he says, "because we still have a marking system. We're going to get rid of that. We're going to have closer student-faculty relationships, with more original work [by students]. We're going to change the social rules. We're going to involve the students more in the control of the college. . . ."

While not yet faced with such arrogant attitudes in his student government, Colorado's Dean of Men James Quigley reports "students don't want to play at student government. Today a regulation must have a reason. And the trouble is a lot of our rules and concepts are carry-overs from previous, outmoded philosophies of what's good for the college students." . . .

A Belief in God, Highly Qualified

Next to his high-school class ring, the first thing today's impressionable college freshman learns he can do without is his old ideas about God.

For most students, it is less a sudden traumatic loss of faith than a gradual fade-out of their adolescent concept of God. This Deity just disappears like a benevolent Cheshire cat. And for the remainder of the undergraduate career, there is little time, inclination, or opportunity to find a more viable replacement. Already pressured when they enter college, forced to fight for grades, required to specialize early and then expected to repeat the whole process through graduate school, today's collegians are less inclined toward theological speculations than earlier generations.

As a result, the question of God is more likely to be passé than problematic and—where it is a problem—more personal than polemical. While three out of four students polled in the *Newsweek* survey acknowledged a belief in God, in many cases the belief may be highly tenuous. Almost 40 per cent of the students said that their experiences in college had made them question their faith. The doubts increase as students grow older. Almost twice as many seniors as freshmen said college had raised questions about their faith. . . .

Confusion usually begins with a student's first encounter with the intoxicating variety of philosophic thought in freshman survey courses. "The middle-class background of most students had the trappings of religion," theorizes . . . Nancy Steffen, the twenty-one-year-old editor of the Stanford University *Daily*, "but their parents were not really religious. As soon as they get to college, a few courses in the history of Western civilization enable them to reject it intellectually."

Only 35 per cent of the students in the survey said they thought it was very important to marry someone who shares the same religious belief. At private nondenominational schools—which tend to be more selective and cerebral—religion seems to mean even less. Forty-one per cent called themselves agnostics or atheists and only 21 per cent said religion would be a very important factor in the choice of a mate. Predictably, religion maintains a strong influence at the private denominational and church-related schools. Only 10 per cent of the students at these colleges classified themselves as agnostics or atheists, while 58 per cent said it was very important to marry someone of the same faith. . . .

At some secular universities, when religion is discussed, it is likely to be a debate over the relative merits of atheism and agnosticism. "The thing to do is to be an agnostic," says Mike Enwall, twenty-two, a married senior and a leading campus politician at the University of Colorado. "That way you always leave a way out if it turns out there is a God."

This tendency to hedge their bets perhaps explains why 75 per cent of the students polled in the *Newsweek* survey expressed belief in God. Today's college generation, which has been coded, carded, and constantly tested and judged, still seems unwilling to discount altogether the possibility of a Final Examiner.

Attitudes toward Sex

Yet this possibility does not appear to affect their worldly manners or morals. A high degree of tolerance pervades campus attitudes toward morality—a mixture of inhibition, realism, cynicism, and jittery concern. The *Newsweek* poll found that two thirds of the boys and girls polled believe that prevailing campus standards encourage promiscuity; and more than four out of five said that their experiences in college had made them take a more tolerant attitude toward those who defy traditional sexual morality. Fifty-eight per cent of the girls said they feel current attitudes make it harder for them to say No. Presumably, the same permissive climate encourages the boys to ask the question more often. And 37 per cent of both the boys and the girls approve the prescription of oral contraceptives in student health centers, a practice already followed at the University of Chicago.

"Premarital sex is accepted," said Allison Hollander, a graduate history student from Washington, D.C., who is now attending a large eastern school, "It's not a mortal sin you'll go to hell for."

Her sentiments reflect the popularity of the "new morality" as preached by many contemporary chaplains. Recognizing that oral contraceptives make fear of pregnancy a poor substitute for principle, the new moralists emphasize that sex is good, but love is better. Without condemning premarital sex as sinful, they offer an ethic of responsible interpersonal relationships. In plain words, the idea is that this will keep sex tied to marriage.

If students across the country acknowledge a new freedom and a new attitude toward sex, many still hesitate to call it a revolution. . . . Beneath the sexual bravado, patterns of traditional morality—or just plain inhibition—are still manifest. Mount Holyoke freshman Elizabeth Bailey confides that college life has taught her sex "is even a more dangerous thing for young people to fool around with than I thought."

Prevalence of Cheating

The most characteristic vice of today's students—not unlike previous generations—is cheating. Nearly two-thirds of all college students interviewed in the *Newsweek* survey said either they or their friends have cheated. More than half of those who admitted cheating cited pressure for good grades as the principal reason. "Business uses your grades as a measuring stick," says Neal Alexander, a graduate student at Georgia Tech. "So good grades are almost essential for success. To some students it doesn't make much difference how they are gotten." . . .

Student Tastes—A Candy Culture

In a mock poll last fall, students at the University of Alabama voted 2 to 1 for Goldwater. But a pre-election get-out-the-vote rally, complete with pretty girls in short skirts, attracted only a handful of enthusiasts. It was a case of bad timing. The rally was scheduled for Thursday, and on Thursdays in Tuscaloosa, young Republicans and Democrats alike stay home to watch *Peyton Place.* "*Peyton Place,*" rally chairman Kay Harris explained, "is the thing most girls get most excited about."

This choice of sudsy drama indicates college students belong to the same vast mid-cult as their parents and younger brothers and sisters. For example, students polled in the *Newsweek* survey said that the movie they had most enjoyed during the last six months was *Goldfinger.* Runners-up were *My Fair Lady, Becket, Tom Jones,* and *It's a Mad, Mad, Mad, Mad World.* Fellini? Bergman? Truffaut? With a few notable exceptions, campus filmgoers don't dig their language.

If serious films have not made much of an impression on the majority of college students, serious paperback books have. In the off-campus "smoke shops" at Syracuse University, the banks of pinball machines that bemused the GI Bill generation have been replaced by racks of paperbacks. Such cerebral and scholarly works as Norman O. Brown's *Life Against Death* and Herbert Marcuse's *Eros and Civilization* sell well—but the best best-seller this year in college bookstores has been *Candy.* Evidently, students whose classroom reading lists are often as thick as college catalogues want entertainment, not enlightenment, from their extracurricular reading.

College tastes are, of course, partly conditioned by the curriculum. Asked to select their favorite author from a list of seventeen, most students named William Faulkner, probably the most studied American novelist, J. D. Salinger second, and Ian Fleming, third.

Fleming was once a fad among the college literati, but when he was discovered by the mass of students, the bond was broken. Similarly, Salinger became *déclassé* when the campus intelligentsia discovered that their kid sisters in junior high had caught on to Holden Caulfield. Coteries on various campuses today read Thomas Pynchon, Ayn Rand, William Burroughs, Günter Grass, and Joseph Heller. British philological fantasist J. R. R. Tolkien has a claque at Harvard, at Carleton there is a minor craze for Apollinaire's pornographic novel *Debauched Hospador,* and at a score of sophisticated schools students have enshrined Alec Leamas, the anti-hero of *The Spy Who Came in From the Cold.*

College students read more magazines—and more comic books —than ever. Individuals are also leaning toward more partisan periodicals, like *The National Review* and *The New Republic.* The iconoclastic *Realist* has appeal for undergraduates at the University of Colorado, and some subscribe to *Playboy* and its fantasy world.

Yet reading itself is nowhere as popular as moviegoing. The *Newsweek* survey shows that more than twice as many students would choose to see a movie than would read a book in their free time. Perhaps that's the reason Fleming is only the third most admired author: students prefer Bond on film rather than in books. . . .

The most avid cult ennobles Humphrey Bogart, pop culture's archetypical anti-hero. Harvard began it all. The Brattle Theater, the original shrine of Bogart campus festivals, now is something like a Grauman's Chinese for the initiate. There is a Club Casablanca bar, Blue Parrot coffeehouse, and wall-size photographs of Peter Lorre, Lauren Bacall, and Bogie himself. The Harvard men not only like great old gangster movies, but real rotten ones, too.

Tastes are not much different at Stanford, which fancies itself as the Harvard of the West. On Sunday night, about two thousand students "flick-out," carrying horns and cowbells, to see cartoons, *Batman and Robin* serials—or *Captain Video*—and a feature, if anyone cares. At Carleton, collegians watch the serial and walk out on the art movie. One recent Sunday, Stanford movie buffs greeted some bad Batman dialogue with shouts of "Author! Author!"

Although folk has not faded completely from the scene, rock 'n' roll is first at many schools. Carleton likes the Rolling Stones, and Wyoming likes late-period Beatle ("Eight Days a Week," not "I Want to Hold Your Hand"). Even disk jockeys have their followers. Collegians in Boston flip for "Woo Woo" Ginsburg, whose trademark is a cacophony of horns, bells, and the "Top 40" sound.

Not every campus is tuned in on pop culture. One University of Texas undergraduate says: "It usually takes a year for a fad to reach here." At Oberlin in Ohio, senior Ed Schwartz says: "Because of the relative isolation of this school, the campus is not oriented to 'in' or 'out' fads. Frankly, I think there is a much greater degree of intellectual honesty in this." And students at Temple University in Philadelphia recently gathered to hear a lecture by Charlton Heston on his movie *The Greatest Story Ever Told*.

Perhaps there is no better measure of student tastes than their pantheon of heroes. According to the *Newsweek* poll, this college generation most admires John F. Kennedy. *Newsweek's* campus correspondents discovered more diverse names. Among them: Lyndon Johnson, Martin Luther King, Albert Schweitzer, George Romney, Hugh Hefner, Dick Gregory, Bob Dylan, Louis Armstrong, Jean Paul Getty, Barry Goldwater, Robert McNamara, Sargent Shriver, William Buckley, Jean-Paul Sartre, and Joan Baez. . . .

Adults' View: Kids Under Pressure

For two millennia or more, the verdict of age on youth had been that of Aristotle: young people have "exalted notions because they have not yet been humbled by life or learned its necessary limitations." But now adults are being forced to change their tune. In the eyes of his elders, today's American college student is a fearsomely intense youngster with his youth already behind him. Exaltation has become a truant from college. By the time America's shining boys and girls get to the campus—as hard-won a piece of real estate as any Tarawa—they have learned more than enough of modern life's awesome limitations to know that exaltation will get them nowhere.

As is always the case when age looks at youth, the eyes of the observers are sometimes misted or jaundiced. Edward Rosenheim, forty-six, a former undergraduate now teaching English at the University of Chicago, says the new college generation is "mirthless and takes itself too seriously, not like my days when one could be a serious student in addition to enjoying himself." Rosenheim could be out of touch, not only with the new generation that has, after all, been known to crack a smile, but with his own generation that probably worked harder than it likes to remember, or admit.

Yet statements and restatements of the same theme of Seriousness are too many and too loud to be ignored. A minister at the University of Iowa, the Rev. Roger Simpson, says the students' great concern is "where they'll fit in a very confused world where the values are changing." Just off campus, the proprietor of Iowa City's Airliner Bar says students in years past knew how to relax. "The ones I see in here all of the time don't last long nowadays." . . .

How, then, do today's vital young oldsters behave? Like generations before, some rebel against authority. "They have less sense of responsibility than any group of teen-agers I have ever worked with," asserts Virginia Hardie, a psychologist at Clemson University in South Carolina. "Their manners are not what they used to be," says Dean Teresa G. Frisch of Wellesley College. "They don't know how to present a boy. They often give only his first name, and they ought to know because what are they going to do when they marry a Foreign Service officer?" . . .

But there are subtle and significant differences in the terms of the new student rebellion. Young people, says Columbia's [Professor of Philosophy Charles] Frankel, "don't really see that what they call the power structure is going to be very easily changed. They don't feel it's very easily movable. There's not much to push against because university presidents, university professors, Presidents of the United States all speak a kind of general liberal language with which students have a great deal of sympathy." At the same time, adds Frankel, "what they push against gives too easily. Parents are likely to talk liberal, too. How can you have a rebellion with nothing to rebel against?" . . .

One of the students' current heroes is Paul Goodman, writer, educator, self-styled anarchist ("I'm a pretty thin hero") who preaches that college administrators should be reduced to the status of janitors and clerks. Goodman calls Berkeley "a historical moment." The leaders of the insurrection, he says, "didn't play it cool, they took risks, they were willing to be confused, they didn't know whether it all would be a success or a failure. Now they don't want to be cool any more, they want to take over." . . .

But contradictions still exist. As soon as the student is ready to be photographed and fixed sharply for all time, he squirms and spoils the picture. Students reject the campus heroes and quest after their own identities. Yes, but they also follow the crowd. "They conform beautifully," reports Bernard Snyder, an Austin clothier whose shops are favored by University of Texas students. Most coeds are style-conscious but tend to conformism, he feels. "If a fashion is new and it fits in with their regular thinking, they really go for it." More often than not, says Snyder, the students "buy something when they want it, and as far as shopping for real bargains, they couldn't care less."

Students are dismayed by the material world around them. Yes, but they're also a part of it. "The prestige of a car is the downfall of some of our students," a California junior-college official says. "I feel so sad sometimes when a student comes in to say he's withdrawing. Then I find out it's because the kid can't make the payments on his car." . . .

In the end, the judgment of age on youth always comes down to educated bafflement. The mother looking at her newborn: what in the world can he be, this wondrous creature with so few defenses and so many chances? The adult looking at the student: what can he possibly be up to, this preposterous unicorn with the graceful gait and eager eye? Yet he seems to know what he wants and how to get it, seems to have every good chance of taking the world for a while and, with help and best wishes, using it well.

CHANGES IN TODAY'S COLLEGE STUDENTS [2]

A lot of the old-time rah-rah spirit has gone out of the colleges in this country.

The college student of today is more serious than the student of a few years ago. He studies harder.

In fact, some college officials are beginning to worry that many students may be taking things too seriously—perhaps even risking their mental health in a frenzied competition for high grades.

This is the picture that emerges from a survey in which members of the national staff of *U. S. News & World Report* talked to administrators, professors and students in more than a score of colleges in all parts of the country. . . .

A parent going back to college today would find many things changed.

Football, while still popular, no longer commands the fanatical enthusiasm among students that it used to—and the football hero is no longer the "big man on campus." The trend now is toward individual sports that a person can continue to enjoy in later life. Art and music are more popular—and more respected.

Fraternities are slipping in importance and prestige. The big dance with the big-name orchestra is becoming a thing of the past. Social life is quieter. There are fewer pranks and fads—such as panty raids and fish swallowing.

[2] From article in *U. S. News & World Report*. 56:66-71. F. 17, '64. Reprinted from *U. S. News & World Report*, published at Washington.

"Maybe now students are just finding a different kind of fun than in my day," says an official at one big state university in the Midwest. "But I don't think they have as much fun as we did."

One factor in the change of college social life and attitudes is this: There are more married students today—as many as 20 per cent are married in some schools.

Even among unmarried students, this is noted: Couples tend to pair off early—and often permanently. Many do not even change partners at dances.

Sex and drinking continue to present problems for the school authorities. Most authorities seem to agree, however, that today's students are wiser about sex and are less likely to drink to excess than past generations.

Politically, today's students appear to be a bit more conservative than their parents were at the same age. Yet many school officials doubt that youngsters now are any less crusaders. They still rally behind "causes." Many actively support racial integration or apply to join the Peace Corps.

Ambitions have changed. Fewer students now plan to go into business for themselves. The tendency is to seek jobs with big corporations. Some authorities express concern that their schools are turning out "organization men."

A rapid growth of graduate schools points up a strong new trend toward more education. For more and more students, a bachelor's degree is only a steppingstone toward a master's or a doctor's degree.

Graduate Dean Richard L. Predmore of Duke University suggests that this might be due to the greatly increased rewards for graduate training in industry, as well as in education.

Some weaknesses are found in today's students, as compared with students of the past. They are often physically weaker, less capable of sustained effort, less skilled in simple mechanical operations. And many professors complain that students have become too blasé, too sophisticated. "They are spoiled by their parents," says one official. "They are given too much too soon."

All in all, however, many educators appear to agree with this judgment by Dr. Harlan Hatcher, president of the University of

Michigan: "The more I get to know today's students, the better I like them. I think they are superior to any group which has ever been here."

More Serious About Study

Nearly all college officials agree that students today are increasingly serious about study. And many officials agree as to the reason. A dean at Colby College in Waterville, Maine, sums it up simply: "Students today are much more serious because they have to be."

"They are expected to produce much more than students of the past," he explained. "The work load they carry is heavier."

At the University of Georgia, a faculty spokesman puts it this way: "Students realize that nowadays you either get education or get left behind. All the talk among them is that today a person is lost, economically, without a lot of education."

President John W. McConnell of the University of New Hampshire says: "Students today are better. Fewer are playboys. They know they can't afford to be. They realize that they must work hard to stay in college and their future depends on doing good work. Competition has become more intense."

"It is not the students who have changed," suggests an administrative official at Bates College in Lewiston, Maine. "It is the world that has changed. If we had seen the need for a college education as clearly as it is apparent today, if we were faced with the heavy competition they face, we probably would have responded in the same way."

Says Dr. David B. Truman, dean of Columbia College, the male undergraduate school at Columbia University in New York City: "Without question, students today are more studious and more serious about intellectual interests. The big change has come in the last thirty-five or forty years. They read a tremendous amount, over and above what they are expected to read for their classes. It is accepted as proper to discuss intellectual interests outside the classroom. You are not considered a 'square' if you do. Why the change? I think there are three reasons. One: We have a more selective student body today. Only the best students are accepted. Two: This is a generation that is desperately looking for answers to their intellectual problems. Third: College work for most of the students here is preliminary to graduate work and professional school. They work harder to qualify for admittance to the professional and graduate schools." ...

Why Some Professors Worry

"These kids today are so darned serious they worry us," says James Denison, administrative assistant to the president at Michigan State University. "There's not one half the rah-rah that I knew in college. There's an intensity, a nervousness we wish they didn't have. We would like to find some way to get them to relax."

"College campuses, like their surrounding society, are becoming centers of intense emotional stress and pressure," says John D. Black, director of the Counseling and Testing Center at Stanford University in Palo Alto, California. "If I read the signs aright, we are in for a vastly increased mental-health problem in our colleges."

"I worry some about the heavy stress on academics today," says an official at the University of New Hampshire. "The freshmen are frightened. I think we are in danger of going overboard, becoming unbalanced. This is one reason we are trying to improve our physical-education setup, hoping to restore some balance."

A West Coast educator expresses this concern: "I wish we could be sure that the students' seriousness is due to a love of learning. But I am afraid that much of it is rather a compulsive competitiveness. I have a feeling that students today are more ulcerous and neurotic. Modern jobs require specific knowledge, and many students are interested in study only to the point that they can measure the benefits. They are so busy learning specifics for complicated jobs that they haven't time for the liberal arts. As a result, we have insecurity in youth and boredom in later years. It's still a rare student who just loves to study. It's not all bad, though, because in this process of competition, they are exposed to a higher quality and greater quantity of subject matter." ...

"When our graduates look for jobs, they seek fast advancement," says Dr. Jack Matthews, dean of students at the University of Missouri. "They want to know how soon they will become a partner in the firm. This is a change. A few years ago they were concerned about fringe benefits. Now what they seem to aim at is to start where most of us older persons got to only after years of work. They want to be able to buy everything right away—all those things we used to save up for years to buy. Students now see an advantage in going to work for big companies. They feel that such companies offer the best chance of making big salaries in a hurry." . . .

A student at the University of Virginia criticizes: "I think most of the boys are here for grades and degrees—not for learning. Take this type we all know who is a top student, and tops in lots of other things, too. He doesn't care at all about learning, about knowledge. He is just out to get ahead. He wants to be vice president of General Motors or something like that—and he'll make it. But I'll bet he has never read a great author outside of class. He knows nothing and cares less about mythology or the true meaning of religion or the development of the culture and philosophy of man. These things won't help him become vice president of the firm."

An official at Virginia halfway agrees: "We are concerned a bit about whether we now are turning out plain 'organization men.' I just don't know. More and more of our graduates do go into big organizations—and become 'organization men.' But who can really blame them for taking one of those jobs? It is not unusual for a graduate to step right out of the university into a job that pays $7,000 a year." . . .

Married Students

Everywhere, you get this report: "Marriage among students is on the increase."

At many schools, about 20 per cent of all students—graduate and undergraduate—are married.

Why? One college official explained it this way: "Many of our married students are graduate students. And we have far more graduate students than we used to have. So it is natural that we should have more married students."

Yet the marriage rate is high among undergraduates, too.

Some officials see a connection between the larger number of married students and the serious attitudes of modern-day students.

Even among the unmarried students, you find a change. The dean of women at a New England college described it this way: "The main change that I think people would notice if they came back to the campus after a long absence is the way the boys and girls pair off. Many couples never date anyone else. If they go to a dance, they do not even exchange dances. I try to tell them what they are missing, but it's no use. It seems to be against the code to switch around very much."

Drinking and Sex Are Still Problems

"Drinking and sex remain as disciplinary problems, but those most closely involved don't see them as any worse problems now than in the past." This was the way an official at one big middle western university summed up the situation—and most other officials seem to agree, in general.

Yet officials—most of them preferring to speak anonymously—found some changes. Said one: "Sex is much more open than it used to be."

Said another: "I suspect that sex is more common today than it used to be. But in terms of students getting into trouble the problem is no worse. One reason, frankly, may be that the students today are more worldly-wise, know how to avoid complications."

On drinking, opinions vary. One official says: "Drinking may be more widespread. Student drinking, in general, reflects the drinking habits of parents. And more adults are drinking, throughout the country."

Another official says: "I don't think there is any more drinking among college students than there used to be—perhaps less. Many are working so hard they don't have time for much drinking."

Some think today's youngsters don't hold their liquor as well as the veterans who attended college after World War II. Others take this view: "There is less heavy drinking. Students seem to exercise more restraint."

Over all, one college official passes this judgment: "I don't see where the morals of today's college students are any different from those of any other generation. I'm certainly not ready to push the panic button."

Another judgment: "Students are just as fine as ever, but they are more at sea about standards and ideals. They are not sure what society expects—what the standards of behavior are."

Politically More Active

A good many college officials see a "conservative" trend in the political views of students.

For example, Dr. John A. Hannah, president of Michigan State University, says: "The students today like to call themselves conservatives. Back in the thirties, students wanted to be liberals."

A Duke University official says: "Here there is a common joke that in an election the faculty would vote left, the students right. I doubt that is a complete truth, but there certainly is more student interest in the right wing now."

A dean at the University of Missouri estimates: "As a group, our students probably are not more conservative than they once were. But we do have a large number of conservatives—and they are more conspicuous."

At San Francisco State College, a representative of the faculty says: "It's hard to label student attitudes, because they are still evolving. But I'd say the basic pattern of most students is middle-class conservative."

However, at Columbia University, an official says: "The large majority of our students are probably a little left of center."

And at Colby College, officials say they can't discern any identifiable trend toward left or right.

Most officials agree on this:

Students today have a lively interest in political issues, international affairs. And today's students show even more interest in "causes."

"The race issue has stirred students all over the country," says one college official.

This comes from a southern university student: "If you're not an integrationist, you're just not one of the crowd any more at this university. It's the social thing to be radical."

"Students are tremendously interested in social issues, particularly in civil rights," reports a dean in a California junior college.

One college president declared: "I'm not convinced that students today are any less crusaders than they used to be. Today their enthusiasm has shifted to civil rights. In my day it was labor relations. Students are still interested in social justice, and they are still willing to make sacrifices. There is a very great interest, for instance, in the Peace Corps."

STUDENTS UNDER STRESS: EMOTIONAL CONFLICTS [3]

A fine old American tradition says that the college years are the best years of our lives, and for many students they still may be. But for a surprisingly large number college has become a time of confusion, misery, frustration and failure.

At the University of Pennsylvania 20 per cent of the students require help from the mental-health service during their college years. At Harvard 25 per cent of the undergraduates consult a psychiatrist or social worker. But these percentages reflect no discredit on Penn or Harvard. A recent poll of six hundred college psychiatrists revealed that about 15 per cent of the students in their institutions seek psychiatric help—while 30 per cent ought to.

The emotional distress that underlies much of present-day college life takes a variety of forms. Campus physicians and

[3] From "The Tormented Generation," by Morton M. Hunt and Rena Corman, free-lance writers specializing in the field of mental health. *Saturday Evening Post.* 236:30-2. O. 12, '63. Reprinted by special permission of *The Saturday Evening Post* © 1963 The Curtis Publishing Company.

nurses often see it as headaches and nightmares, cramps or retching before examination time, fatigue, overweight and forgetfulness. Campus disciplinarians frequently see worse symptoms: drinking and rioting, gambling, outbreaks of cheating on exams, sexual promiscuity. And the police and coroner occasionally see still worse things: the hypodermic syringe and the packet of "snow," the empty bottle marked POISON, the open tenth-story window.

Is this the American dream come true—the dream of a college education for everyone who could benefit from it? Problems and emotional upsets may always have been part of this time of life, but they used to seem trifling, even romantic. Yale men, for instance, have long sung, in charming melancholy, "We're poor little lambs who have lost our way: Baa, Baa, Baa. . . ." Only it isn't so charming now: A recent study shows suicide to be the second most common cause of student deaths at Yale, after accidents. Nationally, suicide is the sixth most common cause of death among people of the same general age group.

What on earth is happening? It would be comforting to discover a single cause for the emotional troubles that afflict nearly a third of our college students—especially if it were one that could be easily overcome. But the fact is that there are several causes—none of them easy to overcome.

Sources of Tension

Some of these causes do, however, have a single origin— ironically enough, the American dream itself. The idea of college for everyone and the importance attached by our society to a college degree—especially the right degree from the right school— have created a whole set of new pressures on our young people.

Since World War II our society has become so college-conscious that teen-agers start to worry years ahead of time about whether there will be room for them in a good school. In the 1930's only a relative handful of high-school seniors took the College Entrance Board Exams; today, when the exams are much tougher, about a million and a quarter students take them. No wonder these youngsters toss sleeplessly at night, develop nervous twitches and shout at their brothers and sisters while waiting for the acceptance letter on which their lives seem to hang.

But being admitted is not the end of the long period of stress. After a brief period of respite things only get worse, since today there is no acceptable alternative to successful graduation from college. "To quit school or to flunk out are no longer reasonable options, as they were when most of us were in college," says Dr. John D. Black, director of the Counseling and Testing Center at Stanford University. "The result is more intense, self-serving competition, more temptation to succeed by hook or by crook, more hostility and anxiety."

All too often these dangerous pressures on the student come from his own well-meaning father or mother. Sometimes this pressure takes the form of parental insistence on a certain college. What the child may want or need is ignored; after all, what does a kid know? The roommate of a boy who had just flunked out of Harvard described such a relationship bitterly. "Bob was a good kid. He'd have made out almost anywhere else, but no, his father had to have a Harvard man for his law firm. So now he's got a Harvard failure. I hope he's satisfied."

Ronald (as we will call him) was another victim of misguided parental ambition. Blond, crew-cut, athletic and good-looking, he seemed perfectly typecast at an Ivy League college. But he didn't act it. He stayed alone in his room a great deal, "to beat the books," he said—though he often smelled of whiskey. By sophomore year he was cutting classes frequently, drinking much more and teetering on the brink of expulsion. One night he punched his fist through a window and needed ten stitches. The physician who sewed him up persuaded him to see the college psychiatrist.

"I never wanted to come here anyway," Ronald admitted to the psychiatrist. "But my father did. He was always bugging me to get another prize or join another club, so I'd be sure to be accepted—to make up for him. And I did. I made the honors list all through high school. And I think half the people in the town I come from knew me, I belonged to so darned many organizations. It's different here, though—all the guys must come from the same prep school or something. They talk their own special language, and a fellow like me can't make it with them. When I used to try, they'd freeze up and look at me down their noses, as if I smelled bad or something. So I started to drink. And then the guys liked me even less and my grades got even worse. I didn't know what to do, so I took another drink."

Ronald talked over his problems with the psychiatrist for half-a-dozen hours, and then decided to transfer to a coed state college. There he was much more comfortable and got along well. He was one of the lucky ones; thousands of others like him never get such help, and quietly sink from view. Others muddle through on their own, at the cost of lifelong psychic damage.

Hard-driving Parents

Parents also put pressure on their children by excessive emphasis on academic success in college. In their eagerness to believe they have a brilliant child, they may fail to hear an average child's cries of distress. Barbara, a slender brunette from Chicago, had been driven hard enough by her parents to get good grades in high school. At an excellent western university, however, she got C's and D's—and even these only by denying herself any time for fun and relaxation.

Feeling guilty and inadequate, she was ripe for trouble. It came in the form of Dan, a boy she fell in love with in her second year. Dan only partly returned the feeling. At once her grades began to slip badly and unfinished assignments piled up. Deeply depressed and full of morbid thoughts, Barbara visited the university psychiatrist. At his advice, she wrote to her parents, asking them to let her take a leave of absence and reconsider her plans in life. Her parents, horrified, wrote directly to the psychiatrist.

"Our Barbara is a brilliant girl," they said, "but she has never even begun to achieve what she is capable of. Instead of leaving now—which would wreck all our plans for her—she should stay, give up that boy and redouble her efforts to make the dean's list. That's *our* idea of psychotherapy!" Barbara, when she learned of this letter, swallowed a dozen sleeping pills. Found in time, she was sent home—a winner of the battle, a loser of the war.

A third way in which parents put pressure on their children is by dictating their choice of career. Hundreds of thousands of unhappy young men and women have suffered through years of training in some field they dislike, because their parents are using them to achieve a vicarious glory. Social worker Bernard Neugeboren, formerly of Yale's Division of Student Mental Hygiene, describes one solution such students unconsciously find: "They assert the right to decide about their lives," he says, "by quietly failing in the work they were forced to take." . . .

Not all the pressures bearing down on today's students are passed on to them by their parents. Indeed, students themselves often generate a lot of their own tensions. "We tell each other again and again how many of us are likely to flunk out," said a senior at MIT. "We pass on all the rumors about how only the top guys get decent jobs. We work ourselves into a real lather and grind away at our books all night. No wonder we get stomach trouble or nightmares."

But students who talk like this are not entirely to blame. They are reflecting the attitude of the society around them—and of their college. For the colleges themselves bear a considerable share of the responsibility for this situation. Most of the best-known schools have been raising their standards of admission, increasing the course requirements, dropping many students who would have sailed through with ease in the 1930's, and encouraging an atmosphere of intense competition.

Moreover, the increased academic competition harms not only the less capable students but many of the extremely bright ones as well. Former Dean Everett Hunt of Swarthmore has said that melancholia seems especially common among exceptionally able students, and Richard C. Carroll, associate dean of Yale College, candidly says, "Somehow, in striving for brighter students—and getting them—we have increased the incidence of emotional instability."

Some gifted people cannot thrive—cannot even endure—in a highly competitive atmosphere; they need one that is more cooperative or permissive or intimate. And many a student who was outstanding in his local public school is shocked and depressed to find, on entering an extremely competitive college, that he has at best a middling sort of talent. "When I came here last year," said a Cornell sophomore, "I'd always had a straight A average in school, and suddenly I was making only C's. It nearly threw me. I was so miserable that I wanted to throw in the towel."

Many capable young people, making this discovery, lack the self-discipline to raise their grades, so they let themselves slide into the discard heap. Others furiously goad themselves on in a single-minded dedication that, at the very least, makes their lives miserable and may lead to more serious trouble. As a girl at the University of Illinois explained in a letter to a friend, "You exist from one assignment to the next, one weekend to the next, living for the time the exam is over—only to start right in on the next one. The pace doesn't let you stop and take a look at *what* you're doing or *why*. That's how I've managed to make the honors list —big deal! I don't even know why I care—or *if* I care."

Although the people who know most about student emotional disorders do not always see eye to eye on the subject, many of them agree with Dean James H. Robertson of the University of Michigan that the chief cause is "personal unreadiness or immaturity." One Yale freshman, who complained he couldn't study and felt awkward on dates, was still getting fried chicken sent by his mother once a week, and cookies in between times. Some college psychiatrists say that the disorder they encounter most often is the kind of immaturity technically known as "personality disorder." People with a personality disorder are often irresponsible, impulsive and lacking in conscience; they do what they please without caring what society will think of them. Typically, they may get drunk, cheat on exams, cut classes, smoke "pot," act rude and vulgar, "sleep around," or build bonfires on the president's front lawn—all without feeling particularly uneasy or guilty.

On some campuses personality disorders account for a substantial portion of suspensions and expulsions, yet there is con-

siderable hope for these youngsters, for time is an effective medicine against immaturity. At Yale the director of the student
mental-health service, Dr. Robert L. Arnstein, said, "We encourage young men of this sort to delay entering college or, if
they have done so and run into trouble, to go on leave and put
in their two years of military service. We once did a follow-up
study of dropouts and found that the majority of those with personality disorders either came back and graduated or finished
college elsewhere or were successfully at work. All in all, a very
high proportion of them turned out relatively well."

"The Identity Crisis"

Another factor contributing to tension on the campus is the
universal problem of growing up, which psychoanalyst Erik
Erikson has called "the identity crisis." Somewhere in the process
of maturing, every young man and woman must figure out and
assume his or her adult identity. This can be especially difficult
for college students because they delay their final decisions for
years, during which they face a bewildering array of new possibilities. And as psychologist Charles McArthur of Harvard says,
"This overlong tentative state of mind is fertile soil for the
growth of neuroses."

There are two main aspects of the collegian's identity crisis.
The first is choice of a career. Though many students find the
freshman year bewildering and difficult, it is during the sophomore year that most undergraduates must decide on a major subject, one that is usually keyed to their future vocation. The frequent result is "sophomore slump"—declining grades and de-
teriorating behavior, the by-product of indecision and perplexity.
For the woman, however, this crisis occurs a second time, in
stronger form, in her senior year, when she has to choose between
marriage and a career. All too often, says Miriam Shelden, dean
of women at the University of Illinois, girls succumb to "senior
clutch"—a frantic grasping at whatever men are nearest at hand,
with resulting marriages that create more problems than they
solve.

Sex is the other main aspect of the identity crisis for college
students. "Am I really a man?" is a painful question for any

youth—particularly when he can answer it only by attempts at seduction or by early marriage (which may force him out of college altogether). As a result, a good many students come to consult the college psychiatrist filled with needless fears of latent homosexuality.

Sex is a somewhat different problem for the girl. She wants to prove her desirability, but she is well aware that premarital sex is not sanctioned by her parents, her church, her school, or even many of her friends. In several recent surveys the majority of college women admit that at times they have "gone farther" than they should have, and that they feel guilty about it. Even if they feel that, because they are in love, it is morally all right to "go all the way," they still conceal what they are doing from their families and even from their roommates, and therefore have to bear the burden of their secrets alone. . . .

Probably the gravest emotional trauma that results from efforts to establish a sexual identity is the unwanted pregnancy which the girl and her boyfriend decide to terminate by abortion. Just how many college girls get pregnant today is unknown, but startling rumors float around on certain campuses. . . .

Sexual problems of all sorts have a special force in college because today so many young people are thrust suddenly into a sophisticated, open-minded environment for which nothing in their background has prepared them. But such difficulties are only part of the larger problem implicit in broadening the college population from a small elite to include boys and girls from nearly all walks of life. "Two or three generations ago," says Dr. Carl M. Grip, dean of men at Temple University, "the undergraduate population was pretty much of a piece. The students came from homes with college backgrounds and a good deal of sophistication. They all had relatively comparable standards and ideas of behavior. Today people of all sorts of beliefs, manners and attitudes are rushing into college and mingling with one another. In a way this is marvelous, but some of them are profoundly shocked and unsettled by their experiences, and many of them suffer keenly."

Submerged in the Crowd

The great influx of students creates yet another hardship: At the larger state colleges and universities school populations are so huge—total enrollments of 15,000 to 20,000 are becoming commonplace—that students are apt to feel lost and ignored. Some exist as virtual nonentities, wretchedly lonely for four years. Others make frantic efforts to become known on campus. As a bright senior at the University of Illinois explained, "You sweat for good grades, you get into all sorts of activities, you poke your way in here and there and run yourself ragged—all to overcome that sense of obscurity and show up as a person."

Is college today really so much more trying than it has always been? Perhaps not for the majority of college students—but it obviously is for a sizable and probably growing minority. "The emotional problems of today's students certainly seem more severe than those of a generation ago," says Dr. Dana L. Farnsworth, psychiatrist and director of the Harvard University Health Services. And Dr. John Black of Stanford is convinced that they are not only more severe but far more common than they used to be.

An indication of this increase is the fact that a number of colleges have set up facilities to treat emotional problems in recent years. Before World War II not more than a dozen colleges had mental-health clinics; today an estimated 125 do—a tenfold increase, even though the total represents only about 6 per cent of the 2,000 institutions of higher learning in this country. It is estimated that some 80 other schools have psychologists on their staffs, and that over 150 have guidance and counseling services which give some attention to relatively simple emotional problems.

Moreover, colleges that offer such services have found that more and more students are taking advantage of them. Harvard inaugurated a Bureau of Study Counsel in 1947 in addition to its long-standing mental-health clinic; each year since then the number of students using the bureau has grown. At the University of Pennsylvania, which opened its mental-health clinic on a full-time basis eight years ago, there was a 25 per cent increase each year in the number of students using it, until a separate study-counseling service was established as well.

Professional psychological help for college students with emotional disorders is undoubtedly valuable. Yet most parents and students will still not find this the answer, primarily because so few schools have such facilities. What, then, can anyone do?

First and foremost, parents should try not to apply damaging pressures to their children—even though they may think they are doing so with the best of intent. Glamour schools, high grades and prestige careers can be genuinely hazardous goals for a student, unless they are really right for him. The mediocre student should avoid the academically tough college, no matter how prestigious it is. The student who is unnerved by competition should seek a college with a relaxed and permissive atmosphere, no matter how bright he is. The shy or retiring student should probably avoid the vast impersonal school; the gregarious, ambitious student might do well to avoid the small egghead liberal-arts college.

Parents should also consider ways of reducing the shock of a late maturing child's first plunge into college life. This might mean that, instead of going out of town his first year, he would go to a school in the vicinity of his home—and plan to transfer elsewhere his second or even third year. It might mean starting at a junior college and stepping up to a larger, more demanding school for the last two years. It might even mean delaying entrance into college for two or three years of work, travel or military service. Or, if he is already in college and having trouble, it might mean voluntary withdrawal on leave for a couple of years.

Our sons and daughters may not be able to echo the words of the Yale graduate of 1928, who said as he strolled through the court of his former dormitory, "I can recall only one unhappy period when I was here. That was in May of my senior year, when I suddenly thought, 'Good Lord, it's nearly over—the best time of my life!' " But neither need they reflect the sentiments of the bitter senior at MIT who recently said, "It's a rat race, a grind, a meaningless ride on a roller coaster. I'm just counting the days till it's over."

IV. THE FACULTY: PRESSURES AND PROBLEMS

EDITOR'S INTRODUCTION

Of all the controversies stirred by the transition underway in higher education, none have been more sharply debated than those concerning the role of the college teacher. What is to be his primary function? Pushing back the frontiers of knowledge? Doing society's basic research? Performing as a hired hand of the Federal Government? Teaching? To most of us it would appear obvious that the primary function of any teacher is to teach. Yet nowadays the standing of faculty members is determined not by excellence in teaching but by excellence in scholarship. "Publish or perish" has become the academic cliché describing this situation.

Like many clichés, it smacks of oversimplification. Good scholarship is certainly one basis of good teaching. But where should the emphasis lie? Today, the young teacher knows that the road to academic success lies in scholarly research and publication rather than classroom performance. He knows that to join the faculty of one of the great, star-studded universities he must himself have become a "star"—and that stars are made through scholarly "contributions to knowledge." Meanwhile, however, will his work in the classroom suffer neglect? Will the intimate contact with students be given over to academic administrators? Will the students themselves trudge through four years on the campus without ever once coming into personal contact with a real, live professor?

These and other faculty problems are the subject of this section. In the first article, a university president seeks to knock the wind out of much of the current criticism by describing three myths about the college teacher. Next, the editor of *Harper's Magazine* launches an attack on needlessly poor teaching at the college level and offers some concrete suggestions as to how the situation can be improved. The following article deals with the so-called "publish-or-perish" issue. In the fourth article, a young instructor at Yale discusses the obstacles that must be surmounted to obtain tenure and the "star system" that governs promotions. And, finally, a Cornell political scientist writes with dismay of the growth of academic bureaucracy and the threat to educational values which such a development represents.

THREE MYTHS ABOUT THE COLLEGE TEACHER [1]

A growing impatience compels me to address myself to three threadbare myths that continue to muddy academic thinking about the nature and function of the American college professor. The first is the appealing myth of St. Mark Hopkins in single and simple communion with THE STUDENT in primitive surroundings. A second is the myth of the ideal teacher as curmudgeonly critic—the unsung and unsinging Socratic scholar. A third is the myth of the teacher-scholar as off-hand administrator.

"The ideal college is Mark Hopkins on one end of a log and a student on the other." How often have we heard or echoed this old saw, sometimes merely underlining the central importance of the gifted teacher in quality education, but often also in deprecation of libraries, laboratories, teaching machines, independent study, and large classes? But what is really being asserted? Who was Mark Hopkins? At what college, to what students, and in what manner did he actually teach what subject? When it recently occurred to me that I could answer these questions but uncertainly, I sought out Professor Frederick Rudolph's admirable book (*Mark Hopkins and the Log: Williams College 1836-1872*, Yale University Press, 1956) and Carroll A. Wilson's witty monograph ("Familiar 'Small College' Quotations, II, Mark Hopkins and the Log," *The Colophon, new ser.* 3 [1938], 194-209). I was unprepared for what I found.

As more sophisticated educators than I may have known already, this statement ascribed to James A. Garfield was uttered in peculiar circumstances, and in somewhat other words. According

[1] From article by Bruce Dearing, president of Harpur College, State University of New York. *Saturday Review.* 47:65-7. Ja. 18, '64. Reprinted by permission.

to Rudolph and Wilson, the episode seems to have developed somewhat as follows. The occasion was a Williams College Alumni dinner at Delmonico's in 1871. As often happens at such convocations, there appeared among the alumni assembled to speak well of themselves, one another, and their alma mater, a representative of the institution; Professor John Bascom had come down from Williamstown to address the gathering. His speech was a bombshell. He asserted bluntly that Williams College was in a deplorable state. The faculty was disintegrating, the students were obstreperous, the libraries and laboratories already essential to genuine higher education in 1871 were nonexistent. Professor Bascom made it clear that he attributed the desperate plight of the institution to the anti-intellectualism, provincialism, indolence, and general laxity of the man who had been for thirty-five years president of Williams College—Mark Hopkins.

It was in response to this attack upon an idol that Garfield coined his famous aphorism. According to Mr. Wilson's persuasive reconstruction, what Garfield actually said was probably "A log cabin in the woods, with a pine bench in it with Mark Hopkins at one end and me on the other is a good enough college for me."

It appears from Professor Rudolph's account that Hopkins' preparation for his academic career was a meager miscellany in the study of law and medicine. Though he lectured principally in moral philosophy and held appointment as professor of philosophy he was proud of the fact that he had read little philosophy. He used Kant only as an example of unintelligibility to hold up to his students' scorn. He had never read either Darwin or Huxley, but nevertheless conducted a thirty-year campaign against what he believed to be their ideas. Despite the enthusiasm of his students—and doubtless Garfield spoke for great numbers of them—the evidence suggests that Mark Hopkins even by the standards of his day, was anti-intellectual, doctrinaire, unread, unlearned, and unashamed.

It is doubtless ungenerous so to assail the reputation of a man whose name has come to symbolize excellence in teaching. It is my purpose to suggest more appropriate models for our emulation.

An ideal college of the mid-twentieth century needs an image other than Mark Hopkins or anyone else on one end of a log and a passive student sitting like a bump on the other. I am not quite ready to settle for Frank Baxter on one end of a coaxial cable and five thousand students on the other, or for a continental classroom making relatively unimaginative use of available teaching resources and devices for an audience of thousands of early risers. Neither do I propose, or fear, that we are headed toward a teacher-student relationship which provides only the confrontation of Skinner teaching machines and students ready to be conditioned.

Even now in our best institutions, libraries provide records, tapes, microfilms and other resources far beyond the capacity of any individual teacher to absorb or purvey. Students in language laboratories learn some things more effectively from tapes and records than they could from an unaided classroom teacher, however gifted. . . . In countless classrooms able teachers are calling upon knowledge of the learning process, and upon their own learning and experience, far beyond anything Mark Hopkins even valued, let alone achieved. In several striking examples, skillful and imaginative instructors in the revolutionized field of mathematics are demonstrating that one teacher can deal effectively with as many as three hundred students on the other end of a logarithm. . . .

The Specter of Socrates

To pervert a well-known and still arresting phrase, "A specter is haunting the academies—the specter (alas, not the spirit) of Socrates." In an essay in the New York *Times Magazine* several years ago, Professor Douglas Bush of Harvard tossed off a now famous aside. In arguing that the colleges and universities should leave off trying to achieve mass education, and happily accept the limitation of educating an academic elite, he said, "Along with that may go another earnest wish, that both administrators and members of departments would abandon the principle of 'publish or perish.' Socrates would never have had a chance at an assistant professorship."

This argument is given witty expression in John Ashmead's satiric "Publish or Perish: Socrates!" in the AAUP [American Association of University Professors] *Bulletin* for December 1955. The burden of Mr. Ashmead's fable is that teachers who publish are hopeless pedants toadying to the dunces (chairmen, deans and presidents) who appoint and promote them, while the genuine teacher is too well occupied with more important things to set pen to paper. It further suggests, quite as insistently, that although that teacher is most stimulating who is most difficult to get along with, his usual fate is exile to some academic Siberia. This bit of academic folklore is depressingly familiar.

Perhaps it would not be amiss to question, as Socrates assuredly would have, the assumptions. Does Socrates indeed represent the ideal teacher? Since Socrates presumably wrote nothing, much depends upon where we get our image of him. If we were to believe Aristophanes, as we probably should not, Socrates was a swaggering fraud. If we credit Xenophon, Socrates was a busybody, adept at everyone's business but his own. For Aristippus, Socrates seems to have been an iconoclast and underminer, systematically attacking the social conventions by which civilization is sustained. Plato's more familiar portrait is doubtless idealized, and the creation as much of artist as reporter. It is not easy for us in our time to put Socrates in perspective, any more than it was for his contemporaries.

As a teacher he is credited with the invention of the widely acclaimed "Socratic method." As I understand this pedagogical method, it is a pose of ignorance eager for instruction, but actually a sophisticated system of relentless questioning. At its best, as it often is in Plato, the Socratic method has much to recommend it to college and university professors. Any careful, utterly serious, courageous and intellectually honest enquiry deserves respectful attention. However, as a method of collegiate instruction, it is expensive and exhausting. Too few of us have the wisdom, patience, intellectual power and honesty, and the sheer physical stamina to use the system consistently and effectively. What is too often done in college classrooms, I suspect, is what Plato allows Socrates to do in many of the dialogues: that is, to present a series of capsule lectures while the other parties restrict themselves to saying in various graceful ways, "You are right, O Master; I cannot disagree." So long as the instructor knows what he is about, his pretense of presiding over a discussion or participating in a vital interchange with the students when he is in fact doing most of the talking may be a harmless fiction, or even a useful stratagem. But when it is the excuse for structureless maundering or puffy pontification, the pseudo-Socrates would far better serve the cause of education by preparing his lectures, or by sending the students out of earshot into the library.

Perhaps a worse perversion of the Socratic pose is the assumption of his role as *gadfly*. Probably in every organization, and most particularly on the campus, there are many who cast themselves as Socratic critics. By inveterate sniping, witty sneers, and sometimes mere churlishness, they may succeed in sabotaging enterprises of great pith and moment, without ever accepting the responsibility of the opposition to propose viable alternatives. The committee member who can speak eloquently against any proposal, but scorns to propose or support any in its stead is maddeningly successful in keeping discussion of academic matters merely academic.

This is an extraordinarily difficult point to make without seeming to encourage supine conformity and to discourage forthright, discriminating and responsible criticism. Unquestionably our colleges and universities need watchdogs concerned about the maintenance of standards. A "loyal opposition" is as essential in an academic community as in any other. But the professor who chooses to define himself as "one who thinks otherwise," needs to assure himself that he is indeed thoughtful, and not merely contrary. He needs to distinguish carefully between maintaining a standard and merely manning a redoubt in some academic Maginot line. Socrates as he is ordinarily imitated is an elusive ideal, and when his shortcomings are emulated as virtues, a little of him goes a long way.

The "Community of Scholars" Myth

The third myth I commend to the skepticism of the teaching profession perhaps is too protean to seize confidently. It relates to the implications and extensions of that favorite academic notion, the educational institution as "a community of scholars." In itself, this concept is due admiration rather than scorn. It asserts the primacy of intellect and enquiry, suggests the unity, consistency, and complementarity of knowledge, and promises the mutual respect and regard so desirable in the several estates of a college or university—students, faculty, alumni, trustees, administrative and maintenance staff. But what the concept too often translates into is something like "the faculty is the college."

One must suppose that the origin of this view is to be found in nostalgia for the universities of medieval Europe, and envy for certain aspects of the modern European universities. In both, viewed from a distance in time and space, it would appear that the professor is supreme; the student deferential, unobtrusive, and peripheral, the alumni vanished, and the administration nonexistent save for a few trifling chores performed casually and intermittently by the scholars themselves. For one who sees a career in higher education as a means for continuing his own study as nearly uninterruptedly as possible, this is perhaps an idyllic vision, and much to be preferred to the troublesome realities of contemporary higher education in the United States.

There are, however, more than a few flaws in the analogy which compares the lot of the American professor so unfavorably with the lot of the British don or the German *Herr Geheimrat* Professor, or their counterparts in other European universities. Most important, but most easily overlooked, is the fact that with very few exceptions, American instructors, assistant professors, and associate professors, and indeed most professors, whatever their gifts, could not reasonably expect ever to attain the exalted rank of professor in a European university with which they like to analogize. In institutions in which there is but a single professor in each major field, the appointment is often a matter, not of mere desert, not of academic politics, but of national politics.

Further, the notion that control of the destinies of the European University is vested solely in the professorial cadre is far from accurate. There is reason to suppose that many if not most of the decisions which in the United States are made by faculties or by local administrations, are in Europe the function of a ministry of education in the central government. I am persuaded that those who most loudly lament the constraints upon the self-government of American faculties would be no more satisfied with the degree of autonomy actually permitted to most European faculties.

Amid the rituals of registration, counseling, housing, assignment and policing, operating dining halls and book stores, assignment of scholarships and loans, placement services, negotiation of government and industrial research contracts, treating with the foundations, the alumni, the press and the accrediting agencies, an American professor or administrative official might well yearn for a simpler task. Unhappily, within our social and educational system we cannot permit ourselves such Graustarkian dreams, however beguiling. We might as well let go of partial analogies between a system designed to educate fewer than one in ten and another which undertakes the task for three to five in ten. The *elite* and *hoi polloi* are different constituencies; a comprehensive institution is different from a single-purpose institution. Relative merits can be argued, the fact of significant difference cannot.

In sum, we need to clear our professional attics of accumulated rubbish, and our colonnades of discredited icons. We cannot afford to exude the elegant platitudes and comfortable orthodoxies of a Mark Hopkins, winning tawdry popularity by telling students what they expect to hear and demanding of them only that they listen approvingly. Neither can we afford to wrap ourselves in a coarse Socratic cloak through whose tatters arrogance and pride are all too visible. We must not too much admire the pseudo-Socrates who imagines he is wise because he finds that nothing pleases him. We can profitably abandon the fantasy of ourselves as European scholar-princes in exile and in chains.

In place of these threadbare myths we may set a new vision of the ideal. We can, for example, find better means of identify-

ing, honoring, and extending the superb teaching of real people
now practicing among us. As students and as teachers we can
recognize and express our discontent with that in our teaching
which is slipshod, archaic, or merely routine and unadventurous.
We will do well not to reject out-of-hand proposed techniques
and devices which are not yet a part of our own experience.
There are few among us who could not profit by learning more
about learning. We should perhaps take a fresh look at what goes
on and what could go on on both sides of the podium in the
lecture hall. We badly need to reexamine the examinations.
Where we have been insisting upon small classes to preserve the
Socratic method of instruction, we should insure that we are not
merely substituting miniature lectures or amiable anarchy for
sinewy dialogue. We may blush that our colleges and universities
are by and large so far behind the military services, industry, and
the public schools in successful adaptation of films, tapes, programed learning, and other devices and techniques available to
the alert and inventive. Our self-limitation to book, blackboard
and bellow, quaint as it may be, is increasingly maladaptive.

And if we need a set of mythical figures to replace these
tarnished ones, let me suggest Prometheus, Hercules, Odysseus,
and Solomon. We need light, vigor, shrewdness and adaptability,
and critical intelligence for the high calling of the teacher in our
land and time.

IS THERE A TEACHER ON THE FACULTY [2]

That muffled snarl you hear is the sound of unhappy college
students enrolling, just about now, for the spring semester. They
are returning to their campuses, by the hundreds of thousands,
with a swelling suspicion that they are being gypped. They are
quite right.

They and their parents are paying dear for an education.
What they expect to get for their money—reasonably enough—

[2] From article by John Fischer, editor, *Harper's Magazine*. 230:18+. F. '65.

is good teaching. In a great many classrooms they are not getting it. This is not because the colleges are poverty-stricken or over-crowded or short of good faculty (although in some cases the situation may be aggravated by all these woes). The harsh truth is that nearly all of our colleges and universities are capable right now of providing far better instruction than they actually put out.

They don't do it simply because our whole academic system is now rigged against good teaching. No faculty member (with rare exceptions) is rewarded if he teaches well, or punished if he doesn't. On the contrary, all the incentives are arranged to divert him away from teaching, no matter how strong a vocation he may have for it, and to penalize him if he wastes too much time on mere students.

During the last few years I have had occasion to talk to hundreds of students, on campus or in my own home; and I cannot remember one of them who was not disappointed, in some degree, by the education he was being offered. Maybe they begin with their expectations too high. The competition to get into good universities has, of course, become enormous. After years of strain and worry, starting in grade school, when a youngster finally makes his way past the flaming sword of the Admissions Officer he expects a good deal of his academic Eden. Then, if he meets indifference, slovenly instruction, and a curriculum only tangentially relevant to his needs, he is likely to get angry.

So are his parents—who are also taxpayers and the prime target of every academic fund-raising campaign. If I read the signs correctly, this smoldering discontent is growing fast. It won't stay bottled up forever; and when it does break into the open, the whole academic world may be in for some distressful days.

Resistance to Reform

Naturally, the more alert college administrators have been aware of this for a long time, and they are worried. Dr. Logan Wilson, president of the American Council on Education and formerly chancellor of the University of Texas, recently warned his colleagues that they had better remember that "colleges were created primarily for students" and that "there is a danger of our becoming indifferent, if not callous, to the sources of discontent and the causes of failure." And President Rosemary Park of Barnard has noted that increasing numbers of students are becoming alienated from college life—no longer rebelling against the campus Establishment but simply ignoring it, including their own undergraduate government, organizations, and publications. Part of the blame, she suggested, lies with the faculty, which no longer has much contact with the students outside the classroom, and all too often only a formal and perfunctory one inside it.

Unfortunately, the administrators seldom can do much about all this. Professors grumble constantly, as we all know, about academic administration—but in fact most universities have less administration per square yard than any other institutions in American life. Typically the president is a sort of Merovingian king, presiding nervously over the savage and powerful barons who run their separate schools, departments, laboratories, and institutes like so many feudal fiefs. He has only very partial command over the university's budget; because of the tenure rule, he cannot fire a lazy or incompetent professor; and his control over what happens in the classroom is marginal. Moreover, even if he had a great deal more authority—comparable, say, to that of a modern corporate executive—he could achieve reforms only very slowly; for the academic world has a granitic, built-in resistance to change. However liberal a professor may be on political or social issues, when it comes to his own professional environment he is almost invariably as conservative as Charles I —believing, indeed, in the Divine Right of the Professoriat to do as it damn well pleases, with a minimum of accountability to anyone, whether president, parent, taxpayer, or student. . . .

It seems unlikely, therefore, that we can hope for any drastic improvement in college teaching to come from either the administrators or the faculties. It will come, if at all, only as the result of outside pressure—from parents, alumni, and the students themselves. Luckily, they have at hand some powerful tools, which they have hardly begun to use. A few ways of putting on the pressure will be noted in a moment.

Why Teaching Is Poor

First, however, it may be useful to take a look at the reasons why so much college teaching is so poor.

The main reason, I am persuaded, is that we do not now have any objective, impersonal method to measure the quality of teaching. It is true that nearly everybody on the campus knows who are the good teachers and who the bad ones; but this information is acquired by a process of hearsay, student gossip, and osmosis. There is no solid, safe yardstick that a dean or department head can use to justify raising the pay of a good instructor, or firing a poor one. He dares not depend on his personal judgment, however sound it may be. That way lie recriminations, accusations of favoritism and injustice, and probably a fight with the American Association of University Professors, one of the most powerful of trade unions.

Consequently, in doling out rewards and punishments the administrator falls back on something that *can* be measured: research and publication. The number of column-inches in learned journals, the pounds of books published, the foundation grants awarded, the prizes won—Nobel, Bancroft, Guggenheim, or a dozen others—these are tangible, indisputable tokens of some kind of academic achievement. (The *quality* of the research or the publications is hardly relevant. After all, an administrator isn't expected to be able to judge whether a finding in biochemistry is really significant, or whether yet another critical evaluation of Henry James adds anything to those already on the shelf.)

Now everybody will agree that research ought to be an important part of academic life. Ideally, we are told, research and teaching go hand-in-hand; the good professor adds to the store of knowledge at the same time he is dispensing it. In practice, alas, things seldom work out that way. So long as research alone pays off, in cash and fame, the temptation to scamp on teaching is almost irresistible. Hence the lectures delivered year after year from notes compiled a generation ago . . . the section men who conduct their classes with unconcealed distaste, begrudging every minute stolen from the lab . . . the perfunctory seminar, the brushed-off questions, the impatient stifling of a student's bothersome zeal. Indeed, human nature being what it is, we should be amazed that so many academics do sweat to teach the very best they can, ignoring self-interest for the sake of the young and their own sense of mission. These rare souls are the saving leaven which can make the college experience worth while (sometimes) in spite of everything. But they are bound to dwindle like the whooping crane if (in Dr. Logan Wilson's words) "the faculty itself regards *relief from teaching* as the chief reward for accomplishment, or as the highest status symbol."

It is idle, however, to rail against the publish-or-perish syndrome, with all its baleful side effects, so long as publication is the only acceptable measure of achievement. A healthy balance between scholarship and teaching probably can never be restored until a reasonably objective yardstick is devised for testing—and rewarding—performance as a teacher. The difficulties are obvious; but, as we shall see, they may not be insuperable.

Teaching the Art of Teaching

Another reason for substandard teaching simply is that college professors don't know how to teach. Aside from a microscopic number who have had some experience in grade or high schools (where formal teacher training is required), nobody on the typical campus has ever had a lesson in learning theory, lecturing techniques, or organization of material for classroom presentation.

This is not a hint (God forbid!) that faculty members ought to be compelled to endure the inanities of the traditional teachers' college. That could prove ruinous, as it does for so many grade- and high-school teachers. But it is not impossible to figure out *good* ways to teach the art of teaching, in as little as one year of intensive work. Already it is being done in a few places—the Master of Arts in Teaching courses at Harvard, Yale, and a couple of other universities, for example. And Dr. James B. Conant has suggested other ways to do it, as part of the regular undergraduate course. Once such training is widely available, it might be sensible to require at least a little of it for all college instructors. In the classroom it would be infinitely more useful than their present compulsory union card, the Ph.D.

Yet another reason for student dissatisfaction is that the best professors are seldom home. Suppose that your Henry decides to go to Halls of Ivy U. because he yearns to sit at the feet of Dr. Grumbacher, The Big Man in Linear Programing, and Dr. McSpivey, the world renowned authority on American history. When Henry gets there, he almost certainly will find that both of them have just left—Dr. Grumbacher to work for the Council of Economic Advisers, Dr. McSpivey to lecture in Thailand on a Fulbright. They won't be back next year either, because when Dr. G. gets the Council straightened out, he's scheduled to take an embassy in an underdeveloped (and probably undevelopable) country, while Dr. M. has a foundation grant to work on his *major opus* in Fiesole, where, by curious chance, some indispensable records have just been located. He will, however, touch home base for one semester after that, before moving on to a stint as historian-in-residence at the White House; but naturally he will have no time for Henry because every one of his precious hours must be devoted to graduate students.

As a matter of fact, Henry will be lucky if he ever sees any full professor of stature, because the academic pecking order is largely determined by the number of consultantships, industrial advisory assignments, off-campus conferences, and traveling fellowships that a faculty member can pick up. Meanwhile, there are plenty of graduate assistants and junior instructors to do the actual teaching. And meanwhile, too, as Dr. Clark Kerr recently observed, "the undergraduate students are restless. . . . There is an incipient revolt against the faculty; the revolt that used to be against the faculty *in loco parentis* is now against the faculty *in absentia.*"

The remedy looks easy. Why doesn't the university simply order the good doctors to stay home and do a little work for a change? Because, if it dared to try such elementary discipline, it would quickly lose its best men. They feel no particular loyalty to that university, or to any other; for in their world, loyalties run to their field of work, not to the institution. And both

Dr. G. and Dr. M. know they can get an offer in a flash from any of a dozen other first-rate schools—with a promise of reduced teaching loads, plus two years leave of absence out of every three for their work on Higher Things.

What might moderate this academic wanderlust is an agreement among all the major universities on a uniform set of rules to govern leaves and teaching obligations. But don't hold your breath. Since the colleges have never yet been able to agree on, and enforce, a code for the hiring of football players, how can we expect them to do so in the almost equally fierce competition for big-name professors? . . .

Some Suggested Remedies

What, then, can be done? Is it possible to set up an acceptable, objective device for measuring—and rewarding—good teaching?

Perhaps the answer lies in that old, reliable maxim of the competitive free-enterprise system: "The customer is always right." Not in its pure form, of course; that would be too shockingly revolutionary for such a conservative industry as American education. But it might be possible to experiment with a watered-down version: "Just possibly, the customer might be right now and then, so let's make a cautious, tentative effort to find out what's on his mind."

In this case, of course, the customer is the student. I am convinced that he is, on the whole, a pretty accurate and fair-minded judge of the quality of teaching he gets. Already his judgment is being felt—in sporadic, unofficial ways—on a number of campuses; and its impact seems to be a healthy one. What I am suggesting, therefore, is simply that the collective student judgment should be sought out systematically, and weighed (along with other factors, including research and publications) in deciding faculty rewards and punishments.

In a crude fashion, this system already is operating in nearly every big university. In some basic fields—European History, for example, or American Literature—the same course will be offered by half a dozen different instructors. If one of them finds his section oversubscribed year after year, while another gets nobody except a few innocents who aren't plugged into the campus grapevine, then you can be fairly certain that the first is a good teacher and the second is not. But, by tacit agreement of the Professoriat, this sort of common knowledge is supposed to be ignored by the administrators. (Not so in the great medieval universities. There, in effect, each student dropped a quarter in the turnstile at the lecture-room door—with the consequence that an Abelard or a Duns Scotus could become a wealthy man. The less brilliant lecturers naturally hated this arrangement, which eventually was trampled to death by the onward march of enlightenment.)

At a few universities—notably Harvard and the University of California at Berkeley—the undergraduates publish their own guides to courses and teachers. Both of these publications are based on questionnaires, filled out confidentially by students enrolled during the previous semester in each of the courses listed. The answers are then tabulated and evaluated, at Berkeley by upper-division and graduate students in the respective departments, at Harvard by the editors of *The Crimson*. It is my impression that both sets of evaluators try hard to be fair, ignoring the comments of soreheads and grudge-nursers. When the evidence is scanty or contradictory, the ratings tend to be cautious; when it is ample, they are brutally candid.

The last issue of the Berkeley *Slate*, for instance, described an English instructor as "one of the brilliant young men who shore up the department; he is a most intelligent and articulate person, easily accessible and very pleasant." In an adjoining paragraph, another man's lectures were reported as "dull, pedantic, and largely irrelevant. . . . Although apparently a technician and a scholar, he is like a used-car salesman selling Tolstoi to a customer he is sure won't buy." Nor are the editors overawed by academic fame. *The Crimson's* thirty-ninth edition of its "Confidential Guide" remarked of the prestigious Dr. Jerome Bruner . . . that he was well-liked, but not as a lecturer, because his lectures were poorly organized and "incoherent." It was even rougher on Dr. J. Kenneth Galbraith, economic polemicist, presidential adviser, and recent ambassador to India.

Obviously, this sort of thing is bound to cause a certain amount of anguish among the faculty. One former teacher (a very good one) told me she could never bear to work on a campus where her performance was thus held up to public scrutiny. But writers, actors, painters, chefs, and automobile manufacturers also suffer when they read reviews of their work—think how the designers of the Edsel must have felt—and yet they somehow continue to operate. Sometimes they even profit from such criticism. Why, then, should teaching be the only important function in our society which is not subject either to criticism or to the appraisal of the market?

After all, Harvard and Berkeley are commonly recognized as two of our best universities, so the unofficial guides evidently have not inflicted any irreparable blight. And students at both places have told me that they find the guides invaluable.

Why, therefore, doesn't every major university have such an undergraduate enterprise? Why, indeed, doesn't the administration encourage them, if the students lack the initiative to start one themselves?

Rating on a Systematic Basis

Better yet, why shouldn't each university set up the machinery for systematic student appraisal of the faculty, on a more thorough and reliable basis than any undergraduate publication can possibly manage? All that would be needed is an unsigned questionnaire, to be filled out by every student in each course at the end of each semester. The results might be evaluated by a tripartite group, including representatives of the faculty, the administration, and graduate students in each department. The ratings need not be published; they could merely be used as one indicator (along with others, including scholarly accomplishment) to guide department heads in deciding on awards of permanent tenure, salary increases, and promotions. The predictable result would be a galvanic increase in the amount of effort invested in good teaching.

[Since this article by Mr. Fischer appeared in early 1965, at least four universities have in fact taken steps to implement this suggestion. At Yale, at the City College of New York, at Cornell,

and at Queens College (New York City), officials have announced their intention to let students have a voice either in
rating the quality of their teachers or in helping to make good
teaching part of the yardstick by which promotions are measured.—Ed.]

All right, I know the standard objections. Many professors
with whom I have discussed this notion argue that: (1) most
students would vote for the merely entertaining lecturer rather
than the sound one; and (2) undergraduates are too immature to
recognize a good teacher. While they are in school they may de-
test old Dr. Slogger, who held their noses so mercilessly to the
grindstone—but in later years they will come to realize that he
was really their benefactor.

I don't believe a word of it. Certainly when I was an undergraduate I knew who my good teachers were (the bad ones too)
and the passing decades have not changed my view in a single
case. Today, moreover, the vast majority of students are more
serious, more rigorously selected, more demanding than in my
day. Few of them go to college—to a good college, at least—
merely for entertainment. Indeed, one of their commonest com-
plaints is against instructors who are *too* entertaining. Here, for
example, are a few typical comments from the Harvard and
Berkeley course guides: "Each lecture was in microcosm the chaos
of the course as a whole . . . anecdotes split off from one another
in seemingly endless progression. Between snatches of the economist's autobiography, students were treated to an unorganized
chain of intriguing thoughts which someday may blossom into
another best-seller." "Entertaining to the point of distraction . . .
low ratings on intellectual stimulation." "A scholarly and articulate Harpo Marx . . . [his lectures] sometimes are virtually all
slapstick and no facts."

But, for academics who are implacably distrustful of their students' judgment, two safeguards might be built into the system.
For one thing, questionnaires might be sent to alumni a year, two
years, five years, and ten years after their graduation. Thus undergraduate "immaturity" could be tempered by blending into
the evaluation the sober afterthoughts of the old grads.

An even better check is the use of outside examiners. In the honors courses at Swarthmore, for example, the final examinations (both written and oral) are conducted by a group of professors imported from other campuses, usually distinguished authorities in their fields. This accomplishes two things, both of them wholesome:

(1) It provides an objective yardstick of teaching ability, since any Swarthmore instructor whose students perform well before the outside examiners, year after year, obviously is doing a good job.

(2) It changes the whole relationship between teacher and students. Automatically he becomes their accomplice instead of their adversary. They know that he is just as eager as they are for all of them to make a good showing. They don't regard him as someone who has to be tricked or flattered, or whose crotchety notions have to be parroted back at him, as so often happens when an instructor writes and grades the exams himself; neither can they suspect him of unfairness or of being "too hard." He and they become true partners in an adventure in learning; and both partners know that their success will be judged jointly, by an impartial and respected authority in the discipline.

Perhaps this explains, in good part, why the teaching at Swarthmore is so widely regarded as about the best going on today anywhere in the country. The only mystery is why the plan has not been adopted everywhere. (It is being used in a few other liberal-arts colleges, but not in any big university that I know of.) The usual excuse is that it is expensive; bringing in a herd of outside examiners costs a lot of money. But I can't imagine any better investment in education.

Money: The Bait for Better Teaching

If innovations of this sort would transform college teaching (as I believe they would), what are the chances that they might be introduced on a fairly large scale?

Most students, and many alumni and parents, seem to feel that there is no hope of changing The System. The typical university is too hidebound, too complacent, too deaf to the needs of its students (and their future employers) to pay any attention to such suggestions. This probably is true—unless each suggestion is accompanied by a firm tug on the purse strings.

For every college and university in America is desperately in need of money. They will have to double their plants and their faculties within the next twenty years to take care of the expected increase in enrollments. Most of this money will have to come from alumni, from parents, and from legislators (who are a good deal more sensitive to the taxpayers' wishes than is the academic world).

So, next time you get an appeal from your alma mater, don't send a check. Send a letter asking what the college is doing to improve its teaching. Does it have any system for appraising teaching ability? At a minimum, why aren't its undergraduates being encouraged to publish something like Harvard's "Confidential Guide to Courses"? Intimate, in a nice way, that you aren't about to make any more contributions until you get satisfactory answers.

If you are a business executive, you almost certainly will be asked during the next six months to make a corporate donation to a new stadium or an aerospace lab or a fund for faculty travel grants. You could say No. You could hint that your firm might, however, be willing to help finance an experiment with outside examiners—or a salary increase for one faculty member in each department who is voted by the students to be the best teacher.

If you are a student, you could raise a little more hell. American undergraduates surely are the most docile in the world—and this may be one reason why they get so much unsatisfactory teaching. I am not urging that they should stone deans, burn classrooms, or riot in the streets, in the academic fashion of Latin America, say, or Iran. But surely they could do a bit more complaining. When teaching is perfunctory, when curricula are arranged primarily for the convenience of the professors, when a good instructor is refused tenure because his publications are scanty, when the Big Men on the faculty spend too much time off the campus, the students really don't have to take it lying down. A few dozen letters to the state's major newspaper, to the foundations whence come those lovely grants, to the legislative appropriations committees—even to the university president—might work wonders. So would a students' report on teachers and courses; it could start as a mimeographed leaflet covering only one department. And why not boo a Bruner, picket a Galbraith, present crowns of laurel to a John Hope Franklin [chairman, Department of History, Brooklyn College], a quart of bourbon to a Royden Dangerfield [professor of political science, University of Illinois]? The possibilities for nonviolent action are infinite—and they could prove a lot more fun than panty raids or beer busts at Fort Lauderdale.

Such tactics, naturally, will not enchant one part of the academic Establishment. Some professors still believe that higher education is an arcane rite which ought to be conducted by (and largely for the benefit of)) its own Sanhedrin, without interference from the peasantry. In the old days, when college was the privilege of a small elite, they could get away with this disdainful posture. But today education is our largest industry. . . . It affects all of us; it reaches deep into every family's pocketbook; it is infinitely more crucial to the nation's future than ever before. Education, as Talleyrand once said of war, has become too serious to leave to the professionals.

Many of the less encrusted academics realize this. They know that the public is bound to have an increasing say in the management of higher education—that the customer has a right to demand a better brand of teaching and that eventually he will get it. These will welcome every pressure for modernization. For in their hearts most of them believe that teaching is a high calling —at least as important as research—and they will rejoice in any change in The System which encourages them to devote to it more of their time and talent.

THE CASE AGAINST "PUBLISH-OR-PERISH" [3]

"Sure he was a great teacher," said one Athenian after Socrates swallowed poison, "but he didn't publish." The joke is old, but it

[3] From "The Publish-or-Perish Policy—Let's Have 'An End On't,'" by Lester E. Hurt, chairman, Department of English, State University College, Cortland, New York. *NEA Journal.* 53:31-2+. D. '64. Reprinted by permission.

has been given fresh bite by a new wave of publish-or-perish sentiment in American colleges.

The recent case of Woodrow W. Sayre, a grandson of Woodrow Wilson, is well-known. The letter dismissing him from the Tufts University faculty after seven years of teaching granted his effectiveness in the classroom but cited his failure to fulfill the "promise of scholarly contribution." By admitting that Professor Sayre was a good teacher, the Tufts administration joined the issue clearly and decisively.

A few simple questions will clarify the publish-or-perish issue still further. What is the prime purpose of a university, or any part of it? What are the major duties of faculty members in accomplishing this purpose? To what extent should the rewards of tenure and promotion depend on performance of these major duties?

The major duty of the faculty members who teach primarily at the graduate level in research-oriented universities is to conduct advanced research and to publish the results. These faculty members, therefore, carry a light teaching load with responsibility for a proportionately small number of students.

The major duty of faculty members in undergraduate colleges, especially those in the humanities, is to teach, and they therefore have teaching schedules of twelve to fifteen hours, with responsibility for 100 to 150 students, or more. This being the case, undergraduate school faculty members ought to be rewarded in terms of how well they teach. To require that they also do substantial publication is to distract their attention from their main duty and to subvert the major function of the institution.

The publish-or-perish boys naturally will bring up the moth-eaten cliché that good teaching is inseparable from research. No one can be a good teacher, their argument goes, who is not constantly engaged in original research—and, presumably, frequent publication, since here is the payoff. This interesting logic rests on two premises: (a) that no one can be a good teacher unless he publishes and (b) that all persons who publish will be good teachers.

Go to, gentlemen. This is humbug, and every experienced teacher knows it. Copeland of Harvard published practically nothing during his teaching career, but his success as a teacher is attested to by hundreds of former students, including scores who became important writers. Every reader has known such a teacher. And every reader has known the teacher who wrote a dozen books but who despised teaching, disliked students, and was rarely available outside class, even for official conferences.

Teaching Is a Full-Time Job

We all admire good teaching. We all admire significant research. But no one has ever shown a necessary and inevitable connection between them. Jacques Barzun, in *Teacher in America*, written twenty years ago, observed that any teacher must keep his reading and his thinking abreast of new developments in his field, but that this does not mean he must also write and publish. Indeed, in many instances it should mean just the opposite.

I am constantly appalled to find how uninformed college professors are outside their own field. I am even more appalled to find how uninformed they often are of matters in their field not pertaining to their particular specialties.

Recently I interviewed a young applicant for a position who came proudly with article in hand but who, in the course of conversation, displayed ignorance of nearly a dozen major works in the area in which he would be teaching. This is hardly surprising when promotion and pay are based largely on publication. Who can blame anyone for rushing into print on Melville before he has read the major criticism on Melville and, for that matter, before he is familiar with all of Melville?

The average undergraduate professor puts in a fifty-hour-week —at a minimum—if he prepares for his classes (I mean *really* prepares for them, including constant revision of his lecture materials), confers with students, corrects papers and examinations thoroughly and judiciously, and plays his part in departmental and college committees and professional organizations. If, in addition, he must publish, then the administration is either running an academic sweatshop or is deliberately tempting the professor to scant his teaching duties.

Every college student knows how the skimping is done. There is the course in which no examinations are given except for the final, which is machine-graded. There is the paper returned with a couple of misspelled words circled, a grade, and the terminal comment, "Watch your grammar"—nothing more. There is the professor who is almost impossible to see and whose conferences, when he makes himself available, are brief and fruitless.

Teachers who commit these malpractices are not necessarily disagreeable or irresponsible. But when their jobs depend on their publication record, they must cut corners wherever they can.

Why the Stress on Publications?

Why do college administrators maintain this fetishism about publications? I believe there are several reasons.

As American colleges were coming of age in the late nineteenth century, numerous American educators were studying in German universities, which considered publication by academicians essential. That they should have become enamored of this and other German academic practices and later established them in this country is understandable.

But it is incredible that all college presidents today do not recognize how unsuitable for American purposes is a practice geared to Germany seventy-five years ago, when higher education was limited to a minute percentage of the national youth.

Along with the German Universität syndrome is the assumption that the experimentation and research carried on by departments of science are equally natural and necessary in departments of art, literature, language, and the other humanities.

Still another reason for "publicationitis" is the desire of small colleges and universities to ape a few large institutions or—more accurately—to ape their graduate faculties who are, properly, research-oriented. By this kind of imitating, many administrators hope to acquire for their institutions national prestige and large grants from foundations and government. All they are doing, of course, is displaying a pathetic snobbishness born out of a sense of insecurity and confusion as to the nature and purpose of their college.

The last and least defensible cause for continued obeisance before the god of publication is that publication offers an easy, "objective" criterion for tenure and promotion. Evaluating an instructor's performance in classroom and conference is admittedly difficult, whereas publication, with its simple, quantitative measurement, does away with the need for agonizing administrative decisions.

In the best of graduate schools, the quality of published articles is also considered. In too many colleges on the make, unfortunately, only quantity counts. For example, the dean of a midwestern college confided to me that his institution had recently promoted a man on the basis of a large quantity of writing which, admittedly, was trivial, shallow, unoriginal, and generally third-rate. His school had proclaimed the doctrine that advancement depended on scholarly "production," and this man had written more than anybody else. To base advancement primarily on publication makes for easy decisions. But it also marks a failure of responsibility, a failure to judge the teacher's performance of his major duty, the thing he is hired to do—to teach. The administration which shirks this responsibility is guilty of cowardice.

Let the Teacher Teach

The average American college is not, cannot be, and should not be primarily a research institution. By every criterion—conditions of employment, faculty assignments, teaching load, community service, public image—it is a teaching institution. The professor who devotes himself wholeheartedly to teaching will have little time left for anything else.

Granted, the teacher who is not constantly engaged in professional study ought to be drummed out of the profession, for a decent college has no place for the laggard and the ignoramus. The most necessary and constructive kind of *study,* however, is often not the kind of *research* that leads to publishable results.

Parents send their children to college to be taught, and undergraduate professors are hired to teach. Let them do it! Any administration that makes faculty survival dependent on publication, in a pathetic and misguided effort to emulate the graduate faculties of a few prestige universities, is guilty of sheer status-seeking hypocrisy. And, to paraphrase Dr. Johnson, let us have an end on't.

THE TENURE PROBLEM [4]

The lessons for junior academic men to be gained from the recent storm over a tenure decision at Yale are not, I think, rightly couched in the language of "publish or perish." To view it in these terms is to see Richard Bernstein, the thirty-two-year-old associate professor of philosophy who was involved, as less than he is, and to treat the point of the students' efforts as less than it was.

Bernstein is regarded by graduate and undergraduate students as an excellent and exciting teacher. He is the editor of an important quarterly in his field, has published some dozen of his own scholarly pieces, and edited volumes of Peirce and Dewey, and has in manuscript the major portion of a book on a large problem of philosophy. So the point that was protested could hardly have been merely that a good teacher but nonproductive scholar was being denied tenure. There were complicated matters of university policy at stake.

A Tenure Appointments Committee in the Humanities, made up of senior faculty from different departments and headed by the Dean of the Graduate School, voted not to grant tenure to Bernstein. But it was quickly learned that the Department of Philosophy, which initiates any action regarding tenure for its members, had submitted a unanimous recommendation for tenure. Though the chairman later described it as "not unconditional," and though the department at the time it submitted its recommendation for tenure added the usual "agreement to abide" by the decision of the committee, one of the voting professors later

[4] From "Yale's Tenure Trouble," by Norman S. Care, instructor, Department of Philosophy, Yale University. *New Republic.* 152:13-14. Mr. 27, '65. Reprinted from *The New Republic,* © 1965, Harrison-Blaine of New Jersey, Inc.

suggested that in such a field as philosophy few men could have been more strongly endorsed than Bernstein was by the department. There immediately followed several days of student activities protesting the committee's decision.

Students React with Protests

It was the implausibility of a unanimous departmental recommendation for tenure, set beside a nearly unanimous committee decision against tenure, that perplexed the Yale public. Criteria for tenure obviously include a man's teaching prowess, the quantity and quality of his research, and his professional standing and promise. A memorandum describing these criteria was sent to faculty members, and it was taken by students to be the force of the department's recommendation that Bernstein satisfied them.

Yale has had a history of unpopular tenure decisions over the past year or so, and the pump was well primed when the decision regarding Bernstein was announced. There was strong faculty support for the efforts of the students. But it was not until the last day of the planned demonstrations that junior members of the philosophy faculty joined the protest in near full force, though certain of them had been active from the start. And the policy of the Department of Philosophy, so far as it had one at this point, seemed to be simply to accept the decision.

The general caution on the part of the faculty is perhaps simply explained. Senior professors who had picked a hazardous path through a system never very precisely structured, and even those who had been brought in with tenure from posts elsewhere, might have been expected to adopt a conservative attitude toward the episode, and even to ignore an opportunity to press for reform. Nontenured faculty perhaps sensed that they could not afford a too vigorous display of support for demonstrations critical of a system upon which their careers were fated to stand or fall anyway.

After several days of protest and discussion, the tenure committee announced its intention to meet "at a later date to decide whether new evidence has been received in the case of Mr. Rich-

COLLEGES AT THE CROSSROADS

ard Bernstein which would warrant reconsideration of its action."
This response was due solely to responsible but vigorous student
action on several fronts. The public demonstrations which drew
the news-media involved chiefly a three-day, round-the-clock
march on the campus, so that Professor Paul Weiss described the
marchers as "peripatetic philosophers." In addition, the campus
newspaper made clear, editorially and by publishing reams of
statements and letters, the points of academic policy at stake.
There appeared student testimonials, near-essays by faculty, ex-
pressions of concern from alumni, and statements from professors
of philosophy at other schools. There were open forums at which
faculty and students spoke, and constant inquiry in the form of
undergraduate and graduate student delegations visited upon administration and faculty. Doubtless these activities contributed to
the possible "new evidence" of which the committee's statement
spoke.

A Question of "Celebrities"?

On the weekend following the committee's announcement
that it would consider whether to reconsider, the senior members
of the Department of Philosophy voted again, this time *not* to
recommend tenure for Bernstein. The department's withdrawing
its recommendation stopped the committee's reconsidering its decision, but it did not end discussion of the propriety of student
demonstrations protesting faculty decisions and university policy.
Conservatives objected that pressures brought to bear by students
(or, as some had it, by the administration) were a "threat to constituted authority." But bringing pressure to bear for the sake of
rectifying an error, or making clear why a certain decision is not
an error, is not only appropriate but required, on a university
campus as elsewhere, to ensure that constituted authority not be
abused.

Aside from the legitimacy of student protest, the affair at
Yale poses certain questions about the form of an academic career.
In "publish or perish" contexts the junior scholar knows what he
must do to earn the academic freedom and economic security
which tenure represents. There is, of course, the evident danger

that his teaching will suffer, rather than his research, since it is the latter which will earn him his place. It is nevertheless clear what the rules of the game are. But in other institutions—and the recent protest must cause Yale to wonder whether it is becoming one—the shape of an academic career is different. It is not an uncommon view that it is in the best interests of a university very concerned with graduate students and research to cultivate as large a roster of academic celebrities as the budget will allow. This view, once it gains currency among the senior members of a faculty, opens the door to a celebrity *policy* for university departments. The ideal becomes, in effect, a department of professionals with high ratings, performing for the chief aim of furthering research in their field.

The Consequences

To say that there exists such a system, or that it is coming to prevail at major universities, is not yet to say that it deserves praise or blame. But it is worth noting its consequences for junior members of a university faculty. One is likely to find departments containing large numbers of staff at top and bottom, with little between. Thus, a department of history in a large university might feature some twenty-five or thirty tenured professors, with a supporting cast of, say, one associate and two assistant professors, no instructors, and some fifty or more graduate teaching aides.

The chances of junior men moving through the ranks to a tenured post are often nil. On this system, when a tenure position is open, more than likely a department will elect to "bring in" an additional celebrity from another school rather than promote a junior scholar, in spite of the good teaching and promising research of the local aspirant. What the junior scholar cannot provide are precisely the attributes of a star.

From this may be drawn a "lesson for education," in Henry Adams's phrase. It is that the terms of an academic career in a celebrity-oriented university are defined in such a way as to make virtually inapplicable the notion of "working one's way through the ranks." In short, it is not reasonable to suppose that one can earn tenure from within. The "publish or perish" game can be won, albeit at some expense to one's students. But the rules of the celebrity game largely preclude a junior scholar's winning at all. One might object that a scholar does not labor to earn tenure, but to gain a glimpse of the truth. But it remains that a junior scholar who is not independently wealthy requires, as a desirable condition of truth-seeking, a post in a university. This is especially so for those in the humanities. Add that young men often have wives, children and debts, and there ensues concern about a system under which a man cannot proceed by good works to a position of security or of freedom: for what the *promising* (as well as unpromising) young scholar is denied in this system is his academic freedom at an institution he may have served for five to ten years. The consequence is a "hired hand" complex among junior scholars, plus the standard set of fruit-picking attitudes which accompany careers involving floating from place to place. One hears such phrases as "riding the circuit" and "being rotated," and constant stories about colleagues' prospects elsewhere.

A Young Teacher's Rewards

The celebrity system does, however, bring with it certain pluses. Most universities in which the system prevails are comparatively exciting places to be. And the system itself affords the junior scholar a curious species of freedom—one generally lacking for those who must publish or perish. Since a member of the supporting cast at an institution in the grips of celebrity policy is in no real position to gain stardom in his home department, he is left pretty much alone. He tends to the students, does some research, has coffee with others of his kind, and occasionally nods to a celebrity in the hall. Perhaps he will send some research to a resident star for appraisal, and hope to receive a comment back in the campus mail. After a few years he will "move out," perhaps to an aspiring state university or liberal arts college, where he will dodge his students to concentrate on the research which will make him attractive enough to cause a department of celebrities to think him worth "bringing in." The results for the education of students may be very similar to those proceeding from the clearer "publish or perish" policy. The students do not win on either system, and it is not clear that research in the humanities does either.

THE GROWTH OF ACADEMIC BUREAUCRACY [5]

Half a century ago Thorstein Veblen concluded in *The Higher Learning in America* that administrative control of our universities was inapposite to many educational values. [For a recent edition of this classic work, see bibliography.—Ed.] Perhaps his own unhappy career was living testimony to this condition. Veblen argued that management's spirit of caution and compromise was not always compatible with the university's needs for free inquiry and disinterest. He deplored the extent to which "the prestige value of conspicuous consumption has come to a greater currency in academic policy." With customary foresight he noted that faculty men might well turn their "best attention in the day's work to administrative duties and schoolmasterly discipline, rather than to the increase of knowledge."

I shall argue that these conditions have been aggravated since Veblen's time. Not only have the costs of administration risen disproportionately, but its underlying values have crystallized until only a major effort can turn them aside.

I am concerned here with conditions in some 45 major universities, which have 40 per cent of all students and about half of all faculty members. Within this group, one must differentiate between some dozen excellent private schools, with their relatively free intellectual climate, and the huge state universities, which despite their vast resources do not always provide a satisfactory intellectual milieu. Even the best of them have built-in limitations that make it extremely difficult to provide a model climate. At any moment some legislative lunatic or thoughtless trustee is likely to invade the campus, demanding a loyalty oath or a winning football team. Their great size and utilitarian ethic harden this situation.

[5] From "University Bosses—The Executive Conquest of Academe," by Robert Presthus, a political scientist at Cornell University. *New Republic.* 152:20-4. F. 20, '65. Reprinted from *The New Republic,* © 1965, Harrison-Blaine of New Jersey, Inc.

As Lazarsfeld and Thielens have shown (*The Academic Mind,* 1960), alienation among faculty members is associated with size: the bigger the school, the more anxiety among faculty men and the more tension between administration and faculty. However muted or ignored, conflict between academic and administrative men is common in our big universities. In their survey of some 375 academic men in nine first-rate universities, Caplow and McGee (*The Academic Marketplace,* 1958), found "an extraordinarily high incidence of conflict." If this is so in the best schools, one can imagine conditions among the majority where administrative control is even more pervasive.

Threat to Intellectual Values

Let me say at the outset that most reasonable men agree that *some* administration is necessary. Nor is conflict necessarily bad. I am concerned, however, with the aggrandizement of university administration and resulting inroads upon intellectual values. Indeed, the well-known drift whereby organizations tend to become diverted from their true ends is painfully apparent in the higher learning. Perhaps the gap between the other-wordly ideals, of the university, its need for diversity and the toleration of ambiguity, and the demands of administration for order and predictability, makes such a displacement inevitable.

One cannot, however, speak of a simple faculty-administration dichotomy. A more complex alignment exists in which the majority of faculty men face a small band of administrators and their faculty allies. A small but significant proportion of faculty men share administrative values of power and prestige. If a mark of intelligence is the ability to accommodate to one's environment, perhaps they are merely validating Darwin's thesis. In any event, they build little fiefdoms within their own departments, meanwhile keeping a keen eye out for wider conquests, since growth is a critical motive.

Firmly place-bound, such men have read every history of the institution; fundamentally conservative, they honor local lore about the superhuman wisdom of its founders. Consummate "locals" whose self-images and career aspirations are tied to their

home base, their values include loyalty, compromise, and a Pan-
glossian optimism. And of these loyalty is paramount. Often
masters of busywork, their major theater of interest and action is
committees, curriculum, planning, memoranda, and academic
pomp and ceremony. In large measure, memberships on university committees are exchanged on a co-optative basis by this
presidium.

This self-selection means that committees will tend to have a
remarkably happy view of the status quo. Faculty salary committees may thus include men with independent incomes, who, like
the conservative who could not understand that liberals may have
felt constrained during the McCarthy era, feel that salaries are
really not bad. And, in any event, no one is really in this game
for money. These men provide a vital link between the sometimes heavy-handed administrator and faculty members who
often have an almost feminine dread of conflict and rather com-
pelling dependency needs. Administrative policies are thus shaped
in academic frames of reference. And since academic statesmen
are often articulate and sophisticated, problems are often defined
in ways that obscure or exclude conflict. An academic freedom
case, for example, rarely occurs, simply because such is rarely included among going premises. The man was not a good teacher;
his research was not really up to par; personal qualities, after all,
are vital; he had been here only six years, etc. Simpler souls who
see issues clear-cut are often out-maneuvered by the parliamentary expertise, experience, and seniority of the home guard.

These academicians *qua* administrators revere our dominant
values of status, prestige and power; they venerate the authority
of knowledge far less than the authority of rank. Their respect
for power and their surprise that others might recognize its con-
figurations, yet not defer to them, are constants. If they are to
some extent used, they collaborate willingly enough, and find
their reward in feelings of shared power and the approval of those
who run the university. They rarely include men who are very
productive academically, and their limited marketability binds
them ever more closely to their administrative masters. As Logan
Wilson notes, "those who disperse largesse are certain to make

dependents, if not create disciples, for much of the academician's immediate welfare, irrespective of his technical competence, depends on administrative policy and how he fits into the scheme of things."

Housekeeping to the Fore

Such men prosper in the academic arena, if only because organizations require all kinds of skills. They enjoy the good will of administrators, who love agreeable pedants who write cheerful books celebrating the pluralism of our democracy and the freedom of our enterprise. Such men instance their practical wisdom by deferring to the marketplace values that characterize most big universities. They endorse the curious phenomenon whereby the true purposes of the university, teaching and research, are more or less subtly downgraded in favor of its housekeeping activities. An equally ironic displacement of roles follows: professors achieve status by becoming administrators, while administrators affect the hallmarks of Academe.

But let us turn to the costs, economic and psychic, of administrative aggrandizement. Higher education now provides our major instrument of social mobility; it produces the trained minds necessary for national growth. . . . Certainly, if its claims for public support are to be honored, the vast resources devoted to it ought to be used as effectively as possible in its job of turning out new knowledge and educated men. One is almost tempted to say that university administration is too important to be left to administrators. My own view is that parents are to some extent shortchanged by the present system, which spends too many resources on educationally irrelevant matters.

First, some examples of bare money costs. Consider the cost of faculty turnover contingent upon the "hire 'em and fire 'em" policies of the larger, mainly state, universities. (More sensitive to the subtle implications of events, the better private universities abhor turnover, except at junior levels, where, prestige being what it is, both individual and institution can benefit. The individual enters the job arena armed with a hallowed name; the institutions enjoy the implication that many are called but few chosen.)

From August 1956 through June 1959, according to official university figures, Michigan State University, one of the public Leviathans, lost over 524 of a total faculty of 1200—a 44 per cent turnover during a three-year period.

While no precise standards exist for "high" or "low" turnover, the loss of over five hundred faculty members in three years is impressive, particularly when one considers the disruption of academic programs and the psychic costs for those who leave as well as for those who remain. Let us assume . . . the cost of replacing each of these men (some of whom, of course, left for reasons not related to our inquiry) at $500, which includes the need to interview at least two, and perhaps several replacements for each post, the faculty time involved in seeing them, etc. Nor should we overlook the salary increment which offers will inspire at their home university. This works out roughly at $250,000 for the three years, enough to provide four new vice presidents, eight senior faculty men, or fifty thousand books. Meanwhile, there are reports that Michigan state government is hard pressed for money.

Another cost is the financial burden imposed by endless administrative offices, some created to administer foundation and Federal research grants, others to fill the status aspirations of university housekeepers, most of whom apparently require vice presidencies to indulge their conceits. As Harvard economist Seymour Harris says:

What is especially striking is the large proportion of the increased costs [of higher education] to be charged to nonacademic salaries; though nonacademic employees were only two thirds as numerous as faculty members, their pay rose so much more that they contributed one third more to the inflation of outlays for institutions of higher learning.

Professors Have to Eat

Costs stem too from the common failure of administrators to make qualitative distinctions among professors, and to reward them accordingly. Bureaucratic standards of seniority and across-the-board pay increments characterize most university reward systems. This, of course, is the easy way out. Administrators pride themselves on their toughmindedness, but this policy, at least, violates that self-image. As a result, other-than-routine increases in rank and income are often denied productive men *until* they present administrators with an ultimatum in the form of an offer from another institution. Alienation follows on the part of that creative minority who largely bring to the university the qualities that honor it. Meanwhile, the mildly cynical job-offer ploy has become part of academic gamesmanship, again adding to costs.

Talented men will be unlikely to trust their careers to a system with these ground-rules. The quaint view of academics as fumbling idealists, unsullied by crass concerns of prestige and income, may provide a rationalizing function, but it is clearly out of context. The number of Ph.D.'s going into academic work has been steadily declining: in 1930, only 18 per cent of them took nonacademic jobs, but by 1956 fully 35 per cent entered other fields. Nine thousand Ph.D.'s are produced each year, but only three out of five now become teachers. In 1953-54, over 30 per cent of new, full-time university teachers had doctorates; only three years later this proportion had dropped to 23 per cent. The remaining 77 per cent may teach long and well; they may be as bright as their mentors; but they are unable to give teaching first priority, harassed as they must be with getting their own degrees and the burdens of family life. Inevitably, they lack experience. As Wellington, reviewing similarly green recruits, remarked, "They may not frighten the enemy, but by God, they frighten me."

This condition results in one of the most pressing issues of university education today: the use of teaching assistants to handle the "sections" into which large undergraduate courses are divided. Such courses meet three times a week; one meeting, the lecture, is handled by an established man (if possible, a "star") in the field. Since the "star" becomes such by research and writing, he cannot teach very much; hence sections are taught by doctoral candidates whose first priority can rarely be students. This is a difficult problem, given the number of students crammed into most major universities. It could be eased, however, by hiring more regular faculty members, whose experience and knowledge would give the student more of what he came for. But such an alternative requires a shift in values away from new buildings, public relations, athletics, and related extra-academic trivia which too often dominate the administrative mind. A fraction of the money spent on the huge piles of bricks and mortar now rising on every campus would be sufficient to ease this problem. Such conditions underlie my belief that parents do not always get full returns for the sacrifices many are making to educate their children.

Growth of Opportunism

Another unhappy result of administrative imperialism is the displacement of intellectual values by those of the marketplace. Power, publicity, consulting service to powerful outside groups, and "practical" research compete strongly with traditional goals. The notion that administrators alone really speak for the university, the ramifications of their roles by all kinds of ceremonial paraphernalia, their monopoly of initiative in university affairs— all tend to weaken academic roles and values. Administrators prefer charming, sensitive, dependent, loyal faculty members and such criteria now compete with professional standards in appointments and promotions. The effects include a subtle demoralization among the most committed of faculty men. Faculty disenchantment weakens the desire to do hard, disciplined work.

The president of the Carnegie Foundation, John Gardner [now Secretary of Health, Education and Welfare], says that the current teaching shortage reflects the "crassest opportunism in grantmanship, job-hopping, and wheeling-dealing" by academic buccaneers who thereby disenchant potential recruits. Since it is the foundations themselves that largely provide the grants which inspire the grantmanship, as well as some of the attractive career alternatives which encourage the job-hopping, the argument seems mildly ingenuous. A better explanation of the teaching shortage is the declining attractiveness of academic work resulting from administrative inroads on the professional independence of highly self-conscious men. Let me offer two examples, both from a major private university. In several instances men recommended for tenure by their colleagues have had this judgment set aside by administrators on grounds that apparently include irrelevant criteria such as personal appearance and conventionality. The point here of course is the wild incongruity of one's professional peers being overruled by men who do not have, and cannot be expected to have, the knowledge to make such judgments. Such practices not only violate the very meaning of the term professional, they reduce talented men to the status of hired hands. They also beg the question: why should bright young men spend eight to ten years in the university preparing for a career with such capricious ground-rules?

Another case involving similarly arbitrary decision-making happened recently at a major private university which spends a great deal of time congratulating itself on the autonomy enjoyed by its faculty. This case, which might be called, "The Perils of Sabbatical Leave," concerns a senior faculty member whose dean removed him from teaching in a basic course, without consultation. The man concerned had an established reputation in his field (at the time of this administrative crime, he was a Fellow of the Social Research Council). The dean's motives were extraprofessional, involving the professor's personality, political values, and his policy toward students. The clash between administrative and academic values is dramatically evident here. The dean was extremely sensitive to student opinion, while the professor was known to demand a great deal from his students. During the eight years he had taught the course, the length of his reading list and the rigor of his marking had become legendary. Some peculiar deficiency of insight, moreover, made him quite independent and even iconoclastic in his teaching and writing. There is some evidence that he had taken seriously the speeches on academic freedom given by university presidents. His greatest blindness, however, concerned his attitude toward university administration, which he failed to honor as the truly vital element in higher education. He apparently believed that administrators were a kind of housekeeper, necessary, yes, but charged mainly with clearing the decks for academic action.

This awkward inability to honor administrative values of power, conventionality, and happy public (student-customer) relations culminated in his purge. In the process, other faculty members received an object lesson in the virtues of obedience and positive thinking. The students are happier, but one wonders if they are wiser. The professor has since left the department for a better post, and the university has lost a highly productive man. Meanwhile, one hears on every hand that good men are hard to find.

How the Europeans Do It

It is at least doubtful whether such values and the offices they inspire have much to do with higher learning. The great European universities have no such top-heavy superstructure. They have even managed to survive for several hundred years without presidents. Perhaps our practices are a cultural artifact reflecting the high overhead costs of business in a rich society. If someone argues that universities today are a "business," which require businesslike leaders, ask him how the Europeans do it.

Parents must be educated. Most of them do not know that much of the university's administrative paraphernalia is not only unnecessary but perhaps detrimental to their children's intellectual growth. I grant that some parents regard higher education as a mobility prize and are not really concerned with quality, but we must try to save them from themselves.

The present concept of the university as an entertainment facility and marriage mart must be changed. The related and apparently endless expansion of state universities under the sophist "democratic" rationale of degrees for everyone can only be slowed by an intelligent public opinion. It *is* possible to differentiate between entertainment and education, and to show that a shining building is less significant than a first-rate library or faculty. Among the big institutions I am generalizing about, physical plant, libraries, athletic fields, etc., are already overdeveloped; it is their investment in human beings, both faculty and students, which lags.

If it is true that one only appreciates what he pays for, an end to the subsidy now given (mainly by faculty members through low salaries) to students in the form of cheap tuition is in order. Students now pay only about 60-70 per cent of the costs of their education. In the prestige schools, at least, they can very well afford to pay the full fare. The income could be used to raise faculty salaries, which are notoriously low, and even more important, to ease the teaching assistant problem.

Insofar as the present administrative mania reflects the thrust toward military science and attending Federal influence (50 per cent of the University of California, Berkeley's annual budget now comes from the Atomic Energy Commission), perhaps we need separate technical universities or centers which would reduce this great and dampening influence upon social studies. The latter are in danger of being suffocated by militarily relevant research.

There is nothing sacred about the present system in which the hard sciences, medicine, and engineering receive the lion's share of resources because they best serve the practical needs of interests outside the university. A more equitable balance ought to be found, in which social and humanistic studies would receive the support they deserve. Curbing the present emphasis on administration would be a good beginning.

EPILOGUE

EDITOR'S NOTE: Much has been written of the trends, problems and controversies in American higher education today. In the heat of battle over costs and direction, over student behavior and faculty performance, we sometimes lose sight of the awesome social and economic impact higher education is having on our lives as individuals and our history as a nation. The concluding article which follows serves to remind us that the value of higher education, in terms of both personal reward and national welfare, has never been higher.

MEASURING THE VALUE OF HIGHER EDUCATION [1]

Education today is in the midst of a great boom. During the past year, some 53 million people—or roughly 28 per cent of all Americans—were enrolled in school. Total cash outlays for public and private schools amounted to an estimated $36 billion, up more than tenfold from $3.4 billion in 1940. Nearly 2.25 million persons were employed as teachers, instructors and professors. It is manifest from such figures that education is one of our greatest industries.

Higher education has been expanding most spectacularly. College enrollments have grown from 1.4 million in 1939-40 to nearly 5 million last year; two out of five persons of college age (eighteen to twenty-one years) were enrolled last year compared with only one out of seven in 1939-40. By the mid-seventies, enrollments are expected to exceed 8 million, with more than half of all eighteen-to-twenty-one-year-olds going to college.

Behind this boom is a growing demand for education. Whereas high school had been a standard of attainment for earlier generations, it is clear that college is now becoming a common goal. Employers have raised their educational standards. Parents know that their children will need more and more schooling to enter

[1] From "Education: Investment in Human Capital." First National City Bank of New York *Monthly Economic Letter.* p 92-5. Ag. '65.

and succeed in occupations and professions that offer better incomes and higher status. They not only spur their sons and daughters to greater efforts in school, but work hard to pay their way through college and graduate study.

But is education being overemphasized? Are too many people going to college? At least until the last decade, many economists seemed to think so. In 1949, for example, Professor Seymour Harris of Harvard warned that the increase in college-trained workers would so flood the job market that "a large proportion of the potential college students within the next twenty years are doomed to disappointment after graduation, as the number of coveted openings will be substantially less than the numbers seeking them."

More recently, however, economists have come up with persuasive evidence that education is not only a good investment for individuals, but is an important key to the nation's economic growth. They regard investment in education as capital embodied in people—"human capital"—that is as important as capital embodied in plant and equipment—or "nonhuman capital."

Human and Nonhuman Capital

That education is an important form of capital is not a new discovery. Economists as far back as the seventeenth century were well aware of the importance of earning abilities embodied in human skills. In his *Wealth of Nations,* Adam Smith explicitly recognized the acquired abilities of people as a form of capital:

> The acquisition of such talents, by the maintenance of the acquirer during his education, study, or apprenticeship always costs a real expense, which is a capital fixed and realized, as it were, in his person. Those talents as they make a part of his fortune, so do they likewise of that of the society to which he belongs.

In the days when slavery and other forms of involuntary servitude were common, scholars apparently had fewer inhibitions about recognizing the capital value of human abilities. In more recent times, even though some economists continued to theorize about human capital, this aspect of economics was generally neglected. With the massive growth of physical capital (plant and

equipment, housing, inventories, etc.), together with the availability of voluminous statistics on capital assets and physical production, virtually all economic studies emphasized the role of
nonhuman capital.

But this one-sided view has led to some serious errors. Thus,
it has been widely assumed that it is the increase in the amount
of capital per worker that primarily explains the growth of productivity per worker in advanced economies. This belief has led
to the use of simple capital-output ratios in planning for economic development of less-developed countries, in which it was
assumed that there was a fixed relationship between the amount
of physical capital invested and the increase in output that could
be expected. Results of such planning have often been quite dis-
appointing in practice.

On the other hand, a number of recent economic studies, have
revealed that investment in human capital—education, on-the-
job training, health, etc.—has played a much bigger role in U.S.
economic growth than previously realized. Thus, in his study,
The Sources of Economic Growth in the United States, Edward
F. Denison calculated that the rising educational level of the
labor force (including managerial and technical personnel) was
responsible for 23 per cent of the growth in real national income
between 1929 and 1957. In contrast, the increase in physical
capital accounted for only 15 per cent, while the general "advance of knowledge" was seen as contributing 20 per cent. Using
a different method but with similar results, Professor Theodore
Schultz of the University of Chicago has estimated that the yield
on our investment in "education capital" over roughly the same
period accounted for about one fifth of the rise in national
output. . . .

Such figures point up the fact that a modern economy does
not depend simply on installing more and better machinery to
attain rising efficiency. Not only are skilled engineers needed to
design and install the improved equipment, but more technically
trained personnel are required to plan and manage production, to
sell and service the product and conduct research for newer and
better products. A growing modern economy also requires more

and more scientists, teachers, doctors and health specialists, advertising and sales people, computer programers and technicians, and mechanics and maintenance workers of all kinds.

Growth in Education

Since the turn of the century the amount of education invested in people has grown at a striking rate. By 1960, the average member of the labor force had spent nearly twice as many days in school as his counterpart in 1930. Since 1890, the proportion of youngsters age fourteen to seventeen in school has risen from 7 per cent to 94 per cent. The percentage of youths eighteen to twenty-one years of age attending college has climbed from 3 per cent to 42 per cent.

While some of this increase in schooling stemmed from the prohibition of child labor, compulsory school attendance laws and the relative decline of agriculture, it primarily reflected the growth of family income. With each succeeding generation, increasing prosperity enabled more and more families to bear the costs of sending their children through high school and in many cases to college. The movement off the farm brought more families into urban communities where educational institutions were readily accessible and greater training was required of those seeking employment.

As parents well know, expanding education costs a lot of money. Since 1900, expenditures for formal education in the United States have risen over one hundred times from $284 million to $34 billion in 1963-64. In contrast to the widely fluctuating growth in physical capital formation, cash outlays for education have been climbing faster and more steadily.

While the rise in education spending reflects increased school attendance, it also stems from the sharp climb in outlays per pupil. Over the period 1900 to 1964, when enrollments in public elementary and secondary schools increased about 2.5 times, expenditures per pupil rose 40 times. Spending for higher education has grown even more dramatically with the 20-fold increase in enrollments during this century. Expenditures per student have multiplied 8 times from $229 in 1900 to $1,920 in 1964, reflecting the rise in faculty salaries and growing expenditures for research and other activities.

In calculating the investment in education, cash outlays for schooling are not the whole story. No less important are the earning opportunities passed up by students in order to go to school. The earnings foregone are a real cost to the student and his family. Professor Schultz has estimated that the percentage of total education costs attributable to earnings foregone by students was 43 per cent for high school, 53 per cent in college and 55 per cent in postgraduate and professional school.

All told the education capital embodied in people has risen much faster than the stock of physical capital. Professor Schultz has calculated that the stock of "education capital" in the labor force as of 1957, measured by its total cost, was 8.5 times its 1900 level. In contrast, the stock of physical capital, as estimated by Professor Raymond Goldsmith of Yale, had risen only 4.5 times since 1900.

And even this estimate of education capital is undoubtedly too low. Changing technology and the increasing degree of specialization require more or less continuous training and retraining, much of it on the job. Professor Jacob Mincer of Columbia has calculated that investment in on-the-job training, measured in terms of costs, is as important as formal schooling for the male labor force and equals more than half of expenditures on formal education. It is estimated that the "on-the-job" capital embodied in the male labor force grew at an annual rate of 5.36 per cent between 1939 and 1957.

Returns on Education Capital

Despite recurrent fears that the growing number of high school and college graduates would glut the labor market, the earnings differentials in favor of better-educated workers have been well maintained. . . . Income statistics indicate that the massive increase in college men has not hurt their relative earnings. In 1939, the average income of college graduates was 57 per cent more than that for high school graduates, and in 1956 and 1961, the relative margin was roughly the same. Demand for college-trained people has kept up with the supply. With the advance of science and technology, the growth of specialized occupations in industry and government has absorbed the increased flow of graduates from colleges and universities. Thus, from 1950 to 1964, while the male labor force increased by 11 per cent, the number of professional and technical workers doubled.

A summary measure of the financial returns associated with education . . . [indicates] that additional years of schooling have been closely associated with substantial increases in lifetime incomes over the past generation. Based on [Herman P.] Miller's calculations [for the United States Bureau of the Census], the average male high school graduate in 1961 could expect to receive one third more in lifetime earnings than a youngster with only an elementary school education. A man who finishes college could expect to make almost two thirds more than the average high school graduate.

There are, of course, many factors in addition to education that account for increased earnings. People who finish college tend to have more drive, innate ability, and physical and financial capacity to get through. These qualities all contribute to earning capacity. Even after allowing for such factors, economists have found that most of the differences in earnings between high school and college graduates remain.

A Highly Profitable Investment

In his *Poor Richard's Almanack*, Benjamin Franklin said, "An investment in knowledge pays the best interest." Though generations of Americans have acted on this belief in getting an education, they have done so without precise knowledge of the likely payoff.

However, in a recent study for the National Bureau of Economic Research entitled *Human Capital*, Professor Gary Becker of Columbia made careful estimates of the return on college education. He found that after allowing for the superior abilities of college graduates, the average rate of return in the form of increased earnings came to more than 12 per cent. This compares with a little over 7 per cent for the average return on total assets in manufacturing. Such high financial returns from advanced education suggest that parents are acting with good foresight in saving or borrowing money to send children to college . . . .

These calculations indicate that education does indeed "pay the best interest." But aside from the private return to individuals, increased education pays large dividends to society as a whole. As noted earlier, Denison attributes 20 per cent of the growth in U.S. national income between 1929 and 1957 to the general "advance of knowledge," which is largely a by-product of educational activities.

Education and National Goals

Economic advancement, of course, is not the sole aim of education. As has always been true, the acquisition of knowledge is an end in itself. The greatest return for the student will continue to be the fulfillment of his individual capacity for intellectual and personal development.

Nevertheless, there is good reason for stressing the economic benefits of increasing education. The goals of the nation, as well as of its citizens, require full development of our resources. As John W. Gardner, the newly appointed Secretary of Health, Education and Welfare, recently pointed out, the demand for educated manpower is a condition of modern life:

> The demand for high-talent manpower is firmly rooted in the level of technological complexity which characterizes modern life, and in the complexity of modern social organization. And more important than either of these is the *rate of innovation and change* in both technological and social spheres. . . .
>
> And the importance of education in modern society is not limited to the higher orders of talent. A complex society is dependent every hour of every day upon the capacity of its people to read and write, to make complex judgments and to act in the light of fairly extensive information. When there is not this kind of base on which to build, modern social and economic developments are simply impossible.

The growing importance of human capital does not mean any downgrading of physical capital. Indeed, accumulation of both kinds of capital are inexorably intertwined in economic progress. The welfare of the nation depends on our increasing investment in both the human capacities of our citizens and the physical capacities of automated facilities and equipment.

From this viewpoint, the sharp increase in young people joining the labor force during the latter sixties may be regarded as a huge addition to the nation's capital stock. They embody more education per person than ever before. Investment in plant and equipment is also rising rapidly. If we make full use of our growing capital stocks in coming years, the world may well see an authentic "great leap forward," American-style.

BIBLIOGRAPHY

An asterisk (*) preceding a reference indicates that the article or a part of it has been reprinted in this volume.

BOOKS, PAMPHLETS, AND DOCUMENTS

American Association of Colleges for Teacher Education. College teachers look at college teaching; report by subcommittee of the Committee on Studies. The Association. 1201 Sixteenth St. N.W. Washington, D.C. 20036 '65.

American Association of University Women. Change and choice for the college woman. (AAUW Journal 80th anniversary issue) The Association. 2401 Virginia Ave. N.W. Washington, D.C. 20037. '62.

Babbidge, H. D. and Rosenzweig, R. M. Federal interest in higher education. McGraw. New York. '62.

Barzun, Jacques. Teacher in America. Little. Boston. '45.

Benjamin, H. R. W. Higher education in the American republics. McGraw. New York. '65.

Boroff, David. Campus U.S.A.; portraits of American colleges in action. Harper. New York. '61.

Bowdoin College. Proceedings of the Symposium on undergraduate environment, October 18-19, 1962. Office of the College Editor. Brunswick, Me. '63.

Bowles, F. H. Characteristics of the modern university. St. Louis University. Office of Public Information. St. Louis, Mo. '63.

Bronowski, Jacob and others. Imagination and the university. University of Toronto Press (for York University). Toronto, Ont. '64.

Carmichael, O. C. Graduate education: a critique and a program. Harper. New York. '61.

*Conant, J. B. Education and liberty. Harvard University Press. Cambridge, Mass. '53.

Cooper, R. M. ed. Two ends of the log; learning and teaching in today's college. University of Minnesota Press. Minneapolis. '58.

Cox, Claire. How to beat the high cost of college. Geis (distributed by Random House). New York. '64.

Diekhoff, J. S. Domain of the faculty in our expanding colleges. Harper. New York. '56.

Dobbins, C. G. ed. Higher education and the Federal Government: programs and problems. American Council on Education. 1785 Massachusetts Ave. N.W. Washington, D.C. 20036. '64.

Earnest, E. P. Academic procession; an informal history of the American college, 1636 to 1953. Bobbs-Merrill. Indianapolis. '53.

Eble, K. E. Profane comedy; American higher education in the sixties. Macmillan. New York. '62.

Fine, Benjamin and Eisenberg, Sidney. How to get money for college. Doubleday. Garden City, N.Y. '64.

Ford Foundation. Toward greatness in higher education: a first report on the Ford Foundation special program in education. Office of Reports. 477 Madison Ave. New York 10022. '64.

Freedman, Morris. Chaos in our colleges. McKay. New York. '63.

Goldsen, Rose and others. What college students think. Van Nostrand. Princeton, N.J. '60.

Goodman, Paul. Community of scholars. Random House. New York. '62.

Gordon, R. E. and Gordon, Katherine. Blight on the ivy. Prentice-Hall. Englewood Cliffs, N.J. '63.

Greene, Gael. Sex and the college girl. Dial Press. New York. '64.

Harrison, G. B. Profession of English. Harcourt. New York. '62.

Henderson, A. D. Policies and practices in higher education. Harper. New York. '60.

Hill, A. T. Small college meets the challenge; the story of CASC [Council for the Advancement of Small Colleges]. McGraw. New York. '59.

Justman, Joseph and Mais, W. H. College teaching: its practice and its potential. Harper. New York. '56.

Keats, John. The sheepskin psychosis. Lippincott. Philadelphia. '65.

Ludden, Allen. Plain talk about college. Dodd. New York. '61.

McConnell, T. R. General pattern for American public higher education. McGraw. New York. '62.

Millett, J. D. Academic community; an essay on organization. McGraw. New York. '62.

National Opinion Research Center. Stipends and spouses; the finances of American arts and science graduate students. University of Chicago Press. Chicago. '62.

Newsom, C. V. University president speaks out: on current education. Harper. New York. '61.

Orlans, Harold. Effect of federal programs on higher education; a study of 36 universities and colleges. Brookings Institution. Washington, D.C. '62.

Rudolph, Frederick. American college and university; a history. Knopf. New York. '62.

Sanford, Nevitt, ed. American college; a psychological and social interpretation of the higher learning. Wiley. New York. '62.

Sasscer, Harrison, ed. New prospects for achievement: Federal programs for colleges and universities. American Council on Education. 1785 Massachusetts Ave. N.W. Washington, D.C. 20036. '64.

Schmidt, G. P. Liberal arts college; a chapter in American cultural history. Rutgers University Press. New Brunswick, N.J. '57.

Selden, W. K. Accreditation; a struggle over standards in higher education. Harper. New York. '60.

Smith, R. W. and Snethen, H. P. Four big years; the importance of selecting the right college. Bobbs-Merrill. Indianapolis. '60.

Stigler, G. J. Intellectual and the market place, and other essays. Free Press of Glencoe. New York. '63.

Stoke, H. W. American college president. Harper. New York. '59.

United States. Department of Health, Education and Welfare. Office of Education. Economics of higher education. Supt. of Docs. Washington, D.C. 20402. '62.

Veblen, Thorstein. Higher learning in America; a memorandum on the conduct of universities by business men. Sagamore Press. New York. '57.
First published in 1918.

Weidner, E. W. World role of universities. McGraw. New York. '62.

Williams, G. G. Some of my best friends are professors; a critical commentary on higher education. Abelard-Schuman. New York. '58.

Wriston, H. M. Academic procession; reflections of a college president. Columbia University Press. New York. '59.

PERIODICALS

AAUP Bulletin. 50:323-6. D. '64. Moral professor in the immoral university. R. W. Edgar.

AAUP Bulletin. 50:327-32. D. '64. Emotional problems of college students: facts and priorities. S. H. King.

AAUP Bulletin. 51:21-4. Mr. '65. Academic freedom and tenure: a report on late notice cases. B. H. Davis.

America. 110:180. F. 8, '64. Tax credit for education.

America. 110:438-9. Mr. 28, '64. Crisis in our colleges. J. F. Meyers.
Reply: 110:722-3. My. 23, '64. J. I. Domínguez.

America. 110:706-9. My. 23, '64. New breed. A. M. Greeley.
Discussion. 110:863-5. Je. 27, '64.

America. 111:178. Ag. 22, '64. Whose backyard? northern students assist Negro voter registration in Mississippi.

America. 111:292-5. S. 19, '64. Religious studies on campus. R. J. Gerber.

America. 111:504. O. 31, '64. Cutthroat competition; public spending for education.

America. 112:414. Mr. 27, '65. More colleges co-operate.

America. 112:451-3. Ap. 3, '65. Are colleges slipping? symposium.

American Education. 1:back cover. D. '64. Enrollment in colleges and universities, fall, '64.

American Education. 1:14-17+. D. '64. New look of campus living. R. C. Weaver.

American Education. 1:30-2. F. '65. What people think about college. W. C. Eckerman and A. Campbell.

American Education. 1:9-11. Mr. '65. College by plan. E. G. Brown.

American School and University. 37:7+. F. '65. Danger flag up for private colleges. A. M. Bloom.

Atlantic. 211:51-5. Je. '63. Higher education in the 21st century. A. C. Eurich.

Atlantic. 213:55-8. Ap. '64. Must the colleges police sex? J. T. Rule.
    Discussion. 213:42+. Je. '64.

Atlantic. 213:84-7. My. '64. Squeeze on the liberal university. J. D. Brown.

Atlantic. 214:96-101. Jl. '64. College students in trouble; emotionally disturbed students. J. A. Paulsen.

Bulletin of the Atomic Scientists. 20:16-19. F. '64. New estate. A. M. Weinberg.

Bulletin of the Atomic Scientists. 21:15-18. F. '65. Fiscal dilemma of academic science. W. V. Consolazio.

*Business Week. p 90-2+. N. 2, '63. Uncle Sam: big man on campus.

Business Week. p 45-6. My. 16, '64. Federal handouts may get skimpier.

Business Week. p 140-50. Je. 6, '64. Personal business; businessmen return to teaching.

Business Week. p 23-4. Je. 20, '64. Sheepskin explosion; bumper crop of incoming freshmen.

Business Week. p 82+. S. 19, '64. Industry research pays student bills.

Business Week. p. 144+. Je. 26, '65. Old college try gets harder.

Changing Times. 18:9-13. Ap. '64. How will you ever pay for college?

Changing Times. 18:6. O. '64. Applying for college; a guide for high school seniors.

Changing Times. 19:7-10. Ap. '65. No, you don't have to go to college.

Changing Times. 19:17-20. My. '65. Colleges that still have room.

Christian Century. 81:500-2. Ap. 15, '64. Clarification at College Park; low moral standards among fraternity members. V. E. Lowder.

Christian Century. 81:601-2. My. 6, '64. Why not three-year colleges? Wesner Fallaw.

Christian Century. 81:1092-4. S. 2, '64. On the campuses. W. L. Thorkelson.

Columbia University Forum. 8:39-44. Spring '65. What's left at Berkeley. W. Petersen.

Commentary. 38:52-5. Jl. '64. Hutchins of Chicago. R. A. Nisbet.

Commentary. 39:39-47. F.; 84-5. Mr. '65. What happened at Berkeley. Nathan Glazer.

Commonweal. 80:359-61. Je. 12, '64. Saving the liberal arts. Paul Goodman.

Commonweal. 81:33-42. O. 2, '64. New debate: Catholic intellectual
life. A. M. Greeley; J. D. Donovan; J. W. Trent.

Commonweal. 81:595-6. F. 5, '65. Money from heaven? question of
spending so much for science.

Commonweal. 81:602-5. F. 5, '65. Behind the protests at Berkeley. J. F.
Boler.

Commonweal. 82:276. My. 21, '65. Minority view: traditions of free
student university expression upheld by Tufts University.

Commonweal. 82:376. Je. 11, '65. Catholics on campus. James O'Gara.

Commonweal. 82:397. Je. 18, '65. Commencement '65; implications of
protests during 1964-1965 academic year.

Consumer Reports. 30:310-11. Je. '65. Guide to college guides.

*Daedalus. 93:1027-300. Fall '64. Contemporary university: U.S.A.
  Reprinted in this book: Frantic race to remain contemporary. Clark Kerr.
  p 1051-70. *Adapted from his* Uses of the university. Harvard University Press.
  Cambridge, Mass. '63.

Ebony. 20:40-2+. Ap. '65. Cash for college careers.

Educational Forum. 27:459-63. My. '63. College graduate—the half-
educated man. L. M. Stratton.

Educational Forum. 29:111-14. N. '64. Faculty speaks. C. Alexander.

Educational Forum. 29:335-42. Mr. '65. Some ideas of a university.
W. D. Templeman.

Esquire. 62:97-100. S. '64. Pressure: buckle under, Winsocki. David
Newman and Robert Benton.

*First National City Bank of New York Monthly Economic Letter.
p 92-5. Ag. '65. Education: investment in human capital.

*Harper's Magazine. 230:18+. F. '65. Is there a teacher on the faculty?
John Fischer.

Harper's Magazine. 230:86-8+. Mr. '65. Good southern universities.
Virginius Dabney.

Harper's Magazine. 230:75-80+. Ap. '65. Good time at UCLA: an
English view. Richard Gilbert.

Harper's Magazine. 230:53-9. My. '65. Salvation on the campus: why
existentialism is capturing the students. J. G. Gray.

Journal of Higher Education. 35:503-6. D. '64. Multiple-campus colleges. P. Sammartino.

Journal of Higher Education. 36:279-83. My. '65. Understanding
junior-college students; proposals for meeting their special needs.
R. M. Bossone.

Liberal Education. 50:517-25. D. '64. Administrator's role in faculty
development. J. W. Hollenbach.

Liberal Education. 51:5-12. Mr. '65. Is there no balm in Gilead? J. W.
Nason.

Life. 56:4. My. 15, '64. Why pick on a fine teacher? case of W. W.
Sayre.

Life. 58:4. Ap. 2, '65. Students: mostly on target.

Life. 58:107-8+. Je. 11, '65. Great grad school gold rush. John Keats.

Look. 28:19-33. S. 22, '64. Class of '68. T. B. Morgan.

Look. 29:36-40. Jl. 27, '65. What happens when Sigma Chi pledges a Negro.

McCall's. 91:98+. My. '64. Rah! Rah! Rah! college for everybody. Lois Dickert and Art Seidenbaum.

Mademoiselle. 59:24+. Ag. '64. Never again, coed; special position of the coed. David Newman and Robert Benton.

Mademoiselle. 59:260-1+. Ag. '64. Swept with confused alarms: psychological climate on campus. Rita Hoffmann.

NEA Journal. 53:11. Ap. '64. Higher education in America. C. P. Snow.

NEA Journal. 53:57-8. Ap. '64. Half-way to where? or the quantity-quality muddle in college education. L. T. Benezet.

NEA Journal. 53:54-6. S. '64. What's new in higher education? excerpt from Higher education: some newer developments, ed. by Samuel Baskin.

NEA Journal. 53:30+. D. '64. Publish-or-perish policy—"the phrase poses a false issue." W. V. O'Connor.

*NEA Journal. 53:31-2+. D. '64. Publish-or-perish policy—let's have "an end on't." L. E. Hurt.

NEA Journal. 54:20-4. Ap. '65. Morals on the campus; a professor and a minister disagree on the present state of student morality. Nevitt Sanford; Arthur Kinsolving.

NEA Journal. 54:29-30. Ap. '65. This year's freshmen: more and better! A. D. Holt.

NEA Journal. 54:55-6+. My. '65. Revolution in British higher education? T. R. McConnell.

Nation. 198:165-7. F. 17, '64. Sex on the campus; evaded problem. L. A. Kirkendall.

Nation. 200:81-5. Ja. 25, '65. Why the students revolt. Bill Ward.
Reply: inside cover. F. 22, '65. Still apathetic. Ken Auletta.

Nation. 200:251-3. Mr. 8, '65. How to make the college of daddy's choice without really knowing anything. O. Palmer.

Nation. 200:266-7. Mr. 15, '65. Protest at Yale.

Nation. 200:639-43. Je. 14, '65. Post-industrial generation: roots of student discontent. M. B. Freedman.

National Review. 14:456. Je. 4, '63. Is going to college too expensive? Russell Kirk.

National Review. 16:864. O. 6, '64. Should tenure go? case of W. W. Sayre. C. M. Curtis.

National Review. 17:241. Mr. 23, '65. Academic order and the humane scale. Russell Kirk.

National Review. 17:411. My. 18, '65. Here we go again. W. F. Buckley, Jr.

National Review. 17:423. My. 18, '65. Politically ignorant college students; recrudescent Communist movement on the campus. Russell Kirk.

Nation's Business. 53:27-8. F. '65. Education's faceless factories shortchange our students. Felix Morley.

New Republic. 152:14-17. My. 1, '65. Berkeley and beyond. Irving Howe.

*New Republic. 152:20-4. F. 20, '65. University bosses—the executive conquest of academe. Robert Presthus.

New Republic. 152:24. F. 20, '65. What's wrong with our students?

*New Republic. 152:13-14. Mr. 27, '65. Yale's tenure trouble. N. S. Care.

New Republic. 152:9. Ap. 17, '65. Teach-ins.

*New York Review of Books. p 15-18. Mr. 11, '65. Special supplement: Berkeley and the fate of the multiversity. S. S. Wolin and J. H. Schaar.

New York Times. p 1+. O. 21, '65. C.C.N.Y. students to grade faculty.

New York Times. p 34. O. 23, '65. C.C.N.Y. students back tenure plan.

New York Times. p 34. O. 23, '65. New student revolt; unhappiness over teachers' neglect culminates in rating of the faculty. F. M. Hechinger.

New York Times. p 29. N. 9, '65. Challenge for colleges; education act helps schools to aid weaker brethren and communities. F. M. Hechinger.

New York Times Magazine. p 14+. Je. 2, '63. Once the professor was a teacher. J. G. Kemeny.

New York Times Magazine. p 93. O. 13, '63. College student in residence. M. R. Feinberg.

New York Times Magazine. p 25+. Je. 7, '64. Academic freedom: how much is there? Andrew Hacker.

New York Times Magazine. p 36-7+. D. 6, '64. College intellectual. 1965 model. David Boroff.

New York Times Magazine. p 76+. Mr. 28, '65. They're not trying to succeed in business; college seniors. Lawrence Stessin.

New York Times Magazine. p 24-5+. My. 9, '65. Vietnam comes to Oregon U; campus protest called the teach-in. Mitchel Levitas.

*New York Times Magazine. p 25+. Je. 6, '65. College grad has been short-changed. Andrew Hacker.

New York Times Magazine. p 25-7+. N. 7, '65. Voice of the new campus underclass. T. R. Brooks.

New Yorker. 41:52-4+. Mr. 13, '65. Letter from Berkeley. Calvin Trillin.

Newsweek. 63:52-6+. Ap. 6, '64. Morals revolution on U.S. campus.

Newsweek. 63:64. Je. 8, '64. Depth vs. breadth; re-evaluation of traditional curriculum.

Newsweek. 63:98+. Je. 15, '64. Big man on campus bigger than ever; class of 1964.

Newsweek. 64:55. Jl. 20, '64. Electronic fathers; computers counsel students.

Newsweek. 64:49. Ag. 3, '64. Aid in the shade; financial aid.

*Newsweek. 65:43-8+. Mr. 22, '65. Campus '65.

Newsweek. 65:86. My. 3, '65. I am very sorry that . . . pressure of enrollment primarily in the East.

Newsweek. 65:105. Je. 14, '65. Divorce, college style.

Parents' Magazine. 38:64+. F. '63. Preventing college crack-ups.

Parents' Magazine. 39:40, 70-1+. F. '64. How not to waste college on girls; with study discussion program. M. S. Smart, Grace Hechinger, and F. M. Hechinger.

Parents' Magazine. 39:66-7+. Ap. '64. Two-year community colleges. Ruth Carson.

Phi Delta Kappan. 46:299-302. Mr. '65. Politics and policies in college admissions. F. E. Crossland.

Phi Delta Kappan. 46:303-6. Mr. '65. Admission to college: policy and practice. D. K. Whitla.

Redbook. 123:58-9+. My. '64. How successful are college marriages? Evan Hill.

Reporter. 30:39-41. Mr. 12, '64. When pure science meets pure politics. D. S. Greenberg.

*Saturday Evening Post. 236:30, 33-4. O. 12, '63. Tormented generation. M. M. Hunt and Rena Corman.

Saturday Evening Post. 237:12+. N. 14, '64. Speaking out: don't send Johnny to college. Hugh Kenner.

Saturday Review. 46:46. N. 2, '63. Future of the university. J. W. Gardner.

Saturday Review. 47:60-1+. Ja. 18, '64. Higher education: fourth branch of government? C. K. Arnold.

*Saturday Review. 47:65-7. Ja. 18, '64. Three myths about the college teacher. Bruce Dearing.

Saturday Review. 47:55-8+. Ap. 18, '64. Can state colleges educate for excellence? Paul Woodring; Bernard Baum.
    Discussion. 47:67. My 16, '64.

Saturday Review. 47:45-6. Je. 20, '64. Must college teachers publish or perish? Paul Woodring.

Saturday Review. 47:57-9+. Je. 20, '64. More on campus mores. D. A. Eldridge.

Saturday Review. 47:52-3. Jl. 18, '64. What kind of excellence? V. R. Alden.

Saturday Review. 48:62+. F. 20, '65. What happened at Berkeley. James Cass.
    Discussion: 48:56. Mr. 20, '65.

Saturday Review. 48:86-7. F. 20, '65. Making of college presidents. V. R. Alden.

Saturday Review. 48:96. F. 20, '65. Does the small private college have a future? Paul Woodring.

Saturday Review. 48:55. Mr. 20, '65. Education in a pressure cooker. Paul Woodring.
　　Discussion: 48:76 My. 15, '65.

Saturday Review. 48:64-5+. Mr. 20, '65. College students: the new breed. J. L. Jarrett.

Saturday Review. 48:65-6. Ap. 17, '65. Who makes university policy? Paul Woodring.

Saturday Review. 48:77-9+. My. 15, '65. Our colleges aren't ready for today's students. Harold Howe, 2d.

Saturday Review. 48:12-14+. Je. 5, '65. Young America's newest vocation; awakening the disadvantaged and the disinterested to their political opportunities and responsibilities. A. I. Waskow.

Saturday Review. 48:59. Jl. 17, '65. Publish or perish; publishing vs. quality of teaching. H. M. Wriston.

Saturday Review. 48:60-1+. Jl. 17, '65. Grass roots of campus freedom. Frederic Heimberger.

School and Society. 91:110+. Mr. 9, '63. Research and the university.

School and Society. 92:85. F. 22, '64. Expectations and responsibilities in higher education. J. F. Ohles.

School and Society. 92:263-4. O. 3, '64. Culture at college. L. W. Norris.

School and Society. 92:284. O. 17, '64. Faculty research policy.

School and Society. 92:286-9. O. 17, '64. University comes of age; adaptation of address, October 4, 1963. N. M. Pusey.

School and Society. 93:139. Mr. 6, '65. Nature of the American college. W. W. Brickman.

School and Society. 93:208. Ap. 3, '65. Sexual behavior of college girls.

School and Society. 93:292-3. Summer '65. Non-academic profile of college freshmen.

School and Society. 93:294-5. Summer '65. Student unrest in U.S. and Latin-American universities.

School and Society. 93:296-7. Summer '65. Some ways toward campus peace. V. A. Rapport.

School Life. 46:42-3. Ja. '64. Professional staff in U.S. colleges. R. M. Walker.

Science. 143:11 Ja. 3, '64. Appropriate function of a university. P. H. Abelson.

Science. 144:491. My. 1, '64. Distribution of Federal research funds. P. H. Abelson.

Science. 144:982+. My. 22, '64. Faculty: new Federal survey shows distribution by field and differences in salaries.

Science. 146:1139-42. N. 27, '64. Politics and higher education; address, June 10, 1964. Eric Hutchinson.
  Reply: 147:823. F. 19, '65. F. S. Barnes.

Science. 147:358. Ja. 22, '65. Teachers as scholars. F. T. Worrell.
  Reply: 147:1087. Mr. 5, '65. R. S. Alexander.

Science. 148:198-202, 346-9. Ap. 9-16, '65. Crisis at Berkeley. E. Langer.

Science. 148:918-28. My. 14, '65. Doctoral feedback into higher education. R. H. Bolt and others.

Science. 148:1177. My. 28, '65. One-sided criticism of university research. P. H. Abelson.

Science. 148:1545. Je. 18, '65. What are professors for? P. H. Abelson.

Science. 149:42-4. Jl. 4, '65. Congress: subcommittee surveys effects of federally supported research on higher education. J. Walsh.

Science News Letter. 85:361. Je. 6, '64. American coeds afraid of hard physical work.

Science News Letter. 87:281. My. 1, '65. Professors' salaries still near bottom of scale.

Senior Scholastic. 84:4T. Ja. 31, '64. Free college after H.S.? concerning report by Educational Policies Commission.

Teachers College Record. 66:322-4. Ja. '65. Is college possible?

Teachers College Record. 66:440-4. F. '65. On publishing and perishing. E. J. Shoben, Jr.

Teachers College Record. 66:620-3. Ap. '65. Berkeley syndrome. E. J. Shoben, Jr.

Time. 83:63. My. 29, '64. Universities adopt-a-school plan; northern university aid in raising Negro college standards.

Time. 84:87. O. 2, '64. Far more than grades; college presidents play up the value of values.

Time. 85:67. F. 26, '65. Giving is growing; private support of higher education.

Time. 85:48. Mr. 12, '65. How to rate a teacher; case of R. J. Bernstein at Yale.

Time. 85:53-4. Je. 25, '65. Womb-clingers; non-students on college campuses.

Today's Health. 43:32-5+. F. '65. Financing your college education. Joan Beck.

*U. S. News & World Report. 56:66-71. F. 17, '64. Changes in today's college students.

U. S. News & World Report. 56:43-6. Ap. 27, '64. Big crisis for nation's youth getting into college.

U. S. News & World Report. 57:52-4. Ag. 10, '64. College bound? you can study now, pay later.

*U. S. News & World Report. 58:55-60. F. 1, '65. Now: crisis for state universities?

U. S. News & World Report. 58:54-5. My. 24, '65. If your daughter wants to go to college . . . .

U. S. News & World Report. 58:88. My. 24, '65. For college grads: no job problem.

U. S. News & World Report. 58:62-4. My. 31, '65. In the new South: the way the colleges are changing.

U. S. News & World Report. 58:53-4. Je. 7, '65. Where Reds are busy on the campuses.

University Quarterly. 19:193-4. Mr. '65. Average professor's time. G. W. Carter.

Vital Speeches of the Day. 31:586-8. Jl. 15, '65. Misuses of the university; anxiety in academe; address June 17, 1965. F. A. Johnson.

Wall Street Journal. p 1+. N. 10, '64. Scorning business; more college students shun corporate jobs, choose other fields. Roger Ricklefs.

Wall Street Journal. p 1+. D. 28, '64. College controversy; some educators claim research surge hurts quality of instruction. F. C. Klein.

Wall Street Journal. p 1+. Mr. 23, '65. Grab that grad! offers rise and rivalry sharpens as recruiters swarm over campuses. R. Martin.

Wall Street Journal. p 1+. Ap. 5, '65. Healthy humanities; liberal arts enrolment soars, belying worries over stress on science. A. L. Malabre, Jr.

*Wall Street Journal. p 1+. Ap. 19, '65. Paying for college. Roger Ricklefs.